Fire Your Therapist

**WHY THERAPY MIGHT NOT BE
WORKING FOR YOU AND WHAT
YOU CAN DO ABOUT IT**

Joe Siegler, M.D.

WILEY

John Wiley & Sons, Inc.

To my parents, Alfred and Rosemarie, who taught me
that the heel of Achilles is the gateway to the sky,
and
To my clients, who are my best teachers.

I do not speak these words, Love speaks them
This subject is something I know nothing about.
You can only tell this story if you are a thousand years old.
What can I know? I am a child of the present.
Yet the child I am is a parasite on the Eternal One
And my union with Him ages me centuries.

—Rumi

CONTENTS

ACKNOWLEDGMENTS

My father, Alfred, smart, funny, generous, loyal, and always there. Creative and successful businessman. Thanks for being unflinchingly loving and supportive of our family and everything that matters. You are my role model. You are the strongest believer in Full Life Centers and this book. You are an amazing friend as well as a great father. The Florida nights out are the best.

My mother, Rosemarie, elementary school teacher, great mother, warm, forgiving, loving, laughing; Holocaust survivor, refugee from Freud's Vienna, eternal optimist, organized, glowing, always there. You taught me never to forget my own idealism, that difference is good, and that working toward greatness is a worthy pursuit. You are the definitive mom. You are my role model.

My brother, Jack, who taught me the importance of managing one's life, of compassion for mistakes, and of awareness that no one has "it" under control.

Bruce Wexler, my book editor and teacher from the beginning of this project. Bruce, it's really all because of you. Years ago you told me there was a book in me. It's now here because of you—your faith, editorial competence, friendship, and being there over the years!

Scott Hoffman, my agent, who invited this book to come into being. You are the best for believing in this book and helping to define its mission. Also thanks to the rest of the team at Folio Literary Management, including Ami Greko, Patty Marriott, Jeff Kleinman, Paige Wheeler, and others.

Christel Winkler and all those at John Wiley & Sons, my publisher, who trusted in me as a first-time author and helped make this book better in so many ways. Christel, thanks for your constant support and encouragement.

I couldn't achieve anything without my spectacular staff at Full Life through the years and now. Thanks to Malado Cisse, who came through Katrina, landed in Chicago to be an awesome multitasking office manager—thanks for being in "a good space" and for your friendship. Tons of thanks to the talented and terrific Full Life coaches Joel Neuberger (it's seventeen years, Joel!), Jenny Koss, Rachel Bickenbach, Lara Polavieja, Michael Trammel, Ilysa Grossman, and others for their past service.

Thanks to all the friends and family who have helped me, Full Life, and this book. A book and a business do not come out of a vacuum and constantly need a circle of advisers and friends. Special mention of my sister, Lori Mausner, for helping in so many amazing ways through the years, helping make things happen that no one else could accomplish—thanks for your friendship and networking, and your invitations and printing business; Andrew Nibouar, for great and always-there friendship and for always encouraging the writing of this book; Gale Zemel, for being the first office manager of Full Life even before the center existed— you were there when no one else was, and I will never forget your contributions; Todd Puckett, for your years of dedication and friendship; Julie Krul, for years of service and friendship; Raman Chadha and April Lane at DePaul for appreciated support, networking advice, and their entrepreneurial rules! Joel Herscher for helping Full Life come into being; Scott Anderson, for providing the amazing Wisconsin country space for writing the original book proposals and for putting the chairs together! Linda Klute for friendship, faith, and more than anyone in the early years helping me to visualize Full Life Centers; my original undergraduate mentor at Penn, William Steinmann, M.D., who is the reason I became a physician and who always encouraged me to blaze my own trail; Sankey Williams, who encouraged me during my fellowship at Penn to define my future; Toby Harris for his branding advice and ideas; Full Life architects Pam Hutter and Araceli Garza, for the amazing inventiveness and innovation of the first Full Life Center; Frank Pieri, for friendship and advice through the years; Will Faber as important colleague, supporter, and friend; Dianna Grant, for your belief in innovative solutions; Mark Shields, Judi Miller, Ken Henriksen, and Kathy Adams, who over time have trusted Full Life to enhance the physician and patient experience; Marcia Shapiro, recent mother and perpetual CEO, who has been there as friend and business adviser in hundreds of ways; Rick Volden, whose encouragement and wisdom never cease; Ernie Weis, for friendship and business support; Jess Boyer, for bringing me to Chicago; Rod Shrader, for friendship, networking and business support; Marty Dolan, whose friendship, class, and competence helped Full Life come into being; Jeremy Kriegel and Gregory Chinlund who have continually succeeded in securing Full Life's brand and for helping in so many ways; Dan Mann, for constant friendship and business advice in the early years; Richard Mausner, for his advice and friendship over the years; Paul Goehner, friend and adviser for decades; Tom Serafine, who has always supported Full Life and all I do; Josh Baran, whose PR wisdom and friendship mattered greatly over decades; Jay Lucas, friend and adviser; Giovanni Lugli, for always being there; Farhad Charmforoosh, for great friendship and contributions to Full Life; Joan Kuehl, as friend and colleague, and for providing the beautiful Amagansett place for writing; Amanda Mausner, for writing inspiration in Paris; Eric Mausner, for writing adventures in D.C.; Amy Wolf, for constant friendship and support for decades; David Mausner, for friendship and contributions, and for always being there; Jonathan Edelman, for great friendship and for always being there no matter what—you have helped in enormous ways—your wisdom, competence, and networking are always appreciated; George Mann, for silver dollars; Gilaad

Matar, for friendship and for always helping and networking; Marla Gordon, for being there; Agnes Krol, for financial wizardry; Agata Strzek, for the environment!; Wayne Johnson, for your creativity and the first Web site; Jean Davis, for your powerful and life-lasting affirmation; Daniel Moser; Siu-Hin Wan; Joe Marconi; Lynne Bredfeldt; Heidi Pearson-Carson; Susan Ross; James McCarthy and staff; Amber Gardner; Emily Mills; Adam Burke; Tiffany Schreiber; Tony Bright; Tim Anderson; Sid Wax; Jan Litvene; Marty Raine-Okubo for infinite friendship; Santos Porras; Lisa Brenner; Joe Flaherty; Henry Dove; Alan Eaks; Joe Camper; Pablo McCabe, Jim Stolz, and Youssef Hasbani, for a great writing space and for your entrepreneurial wisdom—who have all supported me in bringing Full Life Centers and this book into reality.

To the staff at the Standard Hotel in Miami, where most of my writing took place on weekends. Thank you for treating me like gold always and inspiring me with the best multidimensional hotel and spa experience anywhere that inspires visitors to greatness in their lives. Special thanks to the visionary Jason Harler, Erica Fickling, Helena, Fernando, Gail, Paul, Jeorge, Laura, Elwanda, Adam, Mauricio, Miguel, and the entire staff. Thanks to Marcen Morris, for my transportation needs in Florida!

Thanks to God and the Spirit sphere, however defined. In gratitude to Ellen Estrada for helping me realize that, though secular, Full Life is an expression of my spirituality and the belief that each of us has the potential to be a work in progress toward greatness. Thanks and sorry to anyone I neglected to mention because you are appreciated.

Introduction

F*ire Your Therapist* is written for "normal" people who know or suspect that therapy isn't the optimal vehicle for reaching their life goals. By "normal," I mean anyone who doesn't have a serious actively symptomatic psychiatric disorder, such as schizophrenia. You may become depressed every so often; you may be neurotic; you may be convinced that you'll never have a good romantic relationship; and you may believe that your career is a failure. You may feel abnormal because of these issues, but the fact is that you fall within the broad boundaries of normal. And that makes it likely that you need another approach besides therapy to work on these issues.

If you're currently in therapy, you can take advantage of the assessment tool in chapter 4 that will help you determine if and in what ways your therapy is falling short. In chapter 5, I'll also help you weigh the pros and cons of therapy versus coaching so you can look at both comparatively and determine what makes sense for you.

In that regard, I'll discuss my belief that therapy is no longer the treatment of choice if you're normal and how the "talking cure" of therapy is a myth. More to the point, I'll explain why coaching is necessary for behavioral change and life optimization to occur. New, highly effective coaching tools and methods are available, and I'll talk about how you can take advantage of these approaches.

Through coaching and other methods, you can figure out how to transform mediocrity into greatness and an unfulfilled life into one filled with purpose and satisfaction. That is my goal in writing this book, and I hope it is your goal in reading it.

I am fascinated with greatness—great individuals, great leaders, great companies, and great countries. I deeply wonder about what makes some people settle for so little from themselves and from their lives, and then what causes other people to try to be the best they can be in the face of many challenging obstacles. I wonder how some companies aspire to greatness and others just seem to be interested in making money no matter what the cost. I watch some leaders inspire with vision and values while others only care about accumulating power and exerting influence. People can choose to be great in some or all areas of life, and this book is written to help you pursue this goal in the areas of your life that are of interest to you.

More specifically, I hope *Fire Your Therapist* helps you achieve greatness. It will help you do so if you're concerned about both enjoying life in the moment and in your future; if you're willing to put in the time and discipline to develop a life plan and then implement it incrementally. This approach is also different from the vague promises of positive thinking advocates, instead offering a way to create and implement a lasting plan for a better, fuller life. By learning how to enjoy the moment in extreme happiness—also known as nirvana—in combination with strategy and implementation of goals, you can create what you want in your life.

Fire Your Therapist gives you permission to question the value of the therapy, mentoring, or life advice you are receiving. It provides concrete ways to measure whether your life is improving, and it can aid in creating an alternative plan for either boosting the effectiveness of your current approach or modifying it to produce a more fulfilling life.

How This Book Evolved

Over time as a psychiatrist, I discovered that more and more patients were entering therapy who did not fit the classic patient profile. Many of them were not struggling with severe traumatic childhood issues or experiencing severe mental health symptoms of depression, bipolar illness, or psychosis. Instead, they were unhappy because of a series of bad romantic relationships; they were frustrated because of dissatisfaction with their careers; they were seeking a spiritual connection; they were looking for ways to lead a more meaningful and effective life. While their issues may have resembled those of low-grade symptoms of mental illness—unhappiness, anger, even guilt—their problems were much closer to the surface and less intense. These issues they were confronting ranged far and wide, including everything from dissatisfaction with body image, financial problems, bad habits, and mild addictions to wanting a more meaningful life. They were struggling to optimize their ability to have a good life, not just address problems.

In writing this book, I will tell the story of how I learned to help people obtain greater satisfaction in all aspects of their lives. This learning began when I launched a groundbreaking coaching organization called Full Life Centers in the winter of 1999 and went on to build the first specially designed coaching center in the fall of 2002. My own journey from young physician and psychiatrist to founder of this new facility is instructive. During my early years as a physician, I saw my mission and methods expanding with my fascination for truly assisting people to achieve desired changes in their lives. By creating coaching methodologies and new tools for clients, I continued to build on the best of my medical and psychiatric training, and then I found that the synergy of the three disciplines would offer clients a new paradigm and method for working on changing their lives and meeting their goals.

I set out to give people tools to design and implement the life they want to live. Human beings have the unique capability to evolve and change over their lifetime. This book will lay out new methods regarding how people will go about both enjoying and planning their lives.

Interestingly, I began this book ten or so years ago, just as I was forming my new company. At that time I called the book *Wellness as Power*. My idea was that wellness resulted from achieving life balance and optimal performance. At that time, few knew how to help people achieve these life-optimizing goals.

When I started my company, I focused on developing the tools and exercises to enable my clients to achieve these goals. As a result, I delayed working on this book until I could test my concepts in the real world with many real clients. Fortunately, my methods not only turned out to be viable, but they also provided me with compelling substantiation of their effectiveness— evidence you'll find in these pages.

Respect for the Past of Therapy

I hope you will use this book not simply to judge or fire your therapist, but also to influence your own course of life planning and optimization so you can deal successfully with the issues and goals that most concern you.

I have deep respect for the credentials, training, and intentions of most licensed therapists. Their clinical training sets them apart from others claiming to help people, such as coaches, advisers, and mentors. I am a big believer in professional training in a clinical field such as psychiatry, psychology, or social work. I believe that this training combined with coaching creates the best results. How else can a coach know how to navigate all aspects of a client's issues and goals? For example, a client may be in grief from losing his job as a successful executive, he may have some minor heart disease, he drinks a little too much, gambles a little too much, has marital problems, *and* he is extremely motivated to develop the next stage of his career. Only a coach with a clinical background could easily navigate all aspects of this complex client. Increasingly, many people are dealing with similarly complex issues.

Unfortunately, most clinicians today have no coaching training, and most coaches have little clinical training. As much as I respect traditional therapists and have faith in their training and dedication, I'm concerned about their ability to provide normal clients with positive alternatives beyond their training in disease models and methods to implement these alternatives. In the years I have run psychiatric health care systems, I have grown increasingly concerned that the current modalities in all behavioral-health clinical fields are not sufficiently outcome-oriented—they historically have paid little attention to outcomes (besides a few recent schools of therapy such as solution-focused psychotherapy and some practitioners of cognitive behavioral approaches). Therefore, the title of this book is also a call to clinicians to evolve and incorporate coaching modalities.

At the same time, coaches need clinical training. They are dealing with all aspects of a client's life, and they need the training to handle severe or minor addictions or bad habits, symptoms of medical or psychiatric illness, or even issues of self-development.

Predecessors of Coaching: Solution-Focused Therapy, Cognitive Behavioral Therapy, and 12-Step Programs

Right from the start, I want to make it clear that coaching didn't just emerge out of nowhere. Instead, it is the natural evolution of a variety of therapies and methods that came before it. Twelve-step programs began in the 1930s to help people manage alcohol and then other addictions. These were spiritual and behavioral programs that offered people an approach not available in health care services at the time. They were anonymous groups open to the public that provided support to attendees and a sponsor to work on the 12 steps of recovery. Cognitive behavioral therapy was developed to help patients change behaviors by becoming aware of how their thoughts affect their feelings. The development of solution-focused therapy (SFT) attempted to ask questions in special ways that fostered problem-solution on the part of the client. Questions were still mostly dealing with problems and exceptions to them, but at least SFT valued client solutions and client goals. SFT was pioneering in the way it was client-focused as well as goal-oriented, as coaching is today. In a sense, SFT was the beginning of coaching, but still was mainly concerned with the medical model—it acknowledged that there was something wrong to be fixed and didn't deal much with peak performance. It also emphasized how specifically worded questions uncovered client wishes in the same way that coaching does today. However, coaching is not limited to solving problems; often its main accomplishment is enhancement through life planning and optimization.

Coaching as a Response to What People Need

More so now than ever before, the public is questioning the value of traditional methods of therapy. People no longer take it on faith that expressing their feelings and exploring the roots of these emotions will get them "unstuck" as well as cure them of sadness, anxiety, loneliness, career dissatisfaction, midlife crisis, or whatever ails them.

Whether using therapists or other professionals, people often have a mismatch between what they really need and what they're receiving. Too often, one size is meant to fit all. Professionals have a standard approach and use it no matter what an individual's specific concerns and issues are. This is the old paradigm.

The new paradigm involves tailoring a coaching regimen to a client's prioritized issues.

Sometimes you know exactly what you need, but in other instances you may have a more general goal, such as life optimization, or a more general complaint, such as low-grade anxiety or depression.

You can then identify who is in the best position to help you. It may be an individual therapist, a coach, or both. You may choose some mix of therapist, life coach, career coach, dating coach, personal stylist, yoga teacher, masseuse, personal trainer, or physician. In all cases, people need to realize that who they choose to help them should flow directly from what their issues are and what they hope to achieve.

People need new methods that assist them in the proactive design of their optimal life, a concept that does not exist in the medical model of therapy, where all issues are viewed as forms of mental illness. They long for approaches that follow the needs of *clients*, rather than the older traditional models that dictate the plan to *patients*. They want methods that are positive, empowering, and affirming, not judging, top-down in style, and controlling.

Now, with the proliferation of therapeutic and coaching alternatives—life coaching, cognitive and behavioral methods, solution-focused therapy, 12-step groups, employment coaching, dating coaching, men's and women's groups, meditation, and the like—the public has become aware that they don't have to rely on traditional therapy alone. The buzz about wellness and peak performance opens up a new market to life optimization, drawing in people who often are unconcerned with the problems that brought patients to therapists. People are aware of a new potential, an awesome empowerment of self that is attainable with life-enhancement work.

If you're in therapy now, however, it's not always easy to say off the top of your head that coaching is a better option. Too often, people don't know whether their treatment is working. They may feel better one day and worse the next. They set vague goals (or no goals at all), then wonder why they're not making any progress.

They may understand their past, but they're unable to alter the present and the future.

As this book's deliberately provocative title suggests, a new therapeutic paradigm has emerged, and I will explain the elements of this approach and how to use it to live a fuller, more meaningful life. I will draw on my experiences as a psychiatrist and as head of the Chicago-based Full Life Centers, where I have pioneered a multidimensional therapeutic model employing the Spheres of Life Coaching Outcomes System (SOLCOS), which produces desired client outcomes in coaching. There are eleven spheres representing all aspects of life. (See chapter 8 for more information on the Spheres of Life.)

A huge audience exists for coaching—anyone who currently is or has been in therapy, or someone who has never looked at therapy as a possible solution to achieving his or her objectives. Many people are ready to break away from traditional approaches, but they're not sure what to do next. They're wary of quack alternatives. They're often fearful of cutting ties with a therapist on whom they've become close or dependent, even if they don't seem to be making much progress or achieving all their goals. Or they want their therapist to facilitate their life-optimization work, but the therapist is stuck in the old mental illness paradigm and doesn't seem to get it. Or they don't know who to turn to for coaching.

All too often, traditional therapy fails to facilitate change. As good as therapy is at offering people insights about *why* they should change, it doesn't help people overcome their fear of change and the inertia that accompanies it. And it almost never gets involved in the "dirty" hands-on implementation of the client's goals and wishes, as coaching does.

Unfortunately, many times, growth is possible only after people have fired their therapists and found a more involved, more action-oriented approach to their personal work. A big part of the problem is that therapists are convinced that their treatment approach is successful, and within a limited context, it is effective. It's only when people want more than therapy can give them—when they want plans that deliver measurable results—that they turn to coaches.

The Center of the Coaching Universe: Lessons Learned and Shared

In 2002, I opened the first (that we know of) coaching center in the world that was designed specifically for coaching—a place to offer people a uniquely designed, affirming, sensory, and physical space to work on the active design of their lives. With small business loans, using all my savings and credit cards over the years, and the encouragement and support of many important people in my life, this coaching center was born. It was called Full Life Centers and was located in Lincoln Park, Chicago. Bright colors, curved walls, specially selected coaching and business-related retail products, refreshments, abstract paintings, and photography depicting the journeys of our clients are just some of the details that communicate to visitors that they're not in a traditional therapist's or doctor's office. Today, it is truly a place for individuals and organizational leaders to work toward goals and greatness.

Spheres of Life Coaching includes exercises that help clients in their life-optimization process and measure their progress toward goals. I developed these coaching methods so clients could move beyond talk. I'll discuss the spheres in detail in the coming chapters, but for now, understand that they provide clients with the opportunity to address challenges and opportunity in all aspects of their lives—not just in the sphere of Self, which is the main domain of traditional therapy. I'll share stories from some of the thousands of clients who have used our coaching approach, demonstrating the impact of our coaching system on a diverse group of people with an equally diverse set of life-optimizing goals.

These stories, combined with the book's tips and tools, should help you take advantage of all the possibilities coaching holds. Whether you want to transition from therapy to coaching or understand how to find a coach, this book will provide what you need.

If any client stories in this book appear to be a real person, that is simply because each is a composite of many different people. The names are fictitious, and they are not representative of any single client—instead they are a blend of thousands of clients over the past twenty-five years.

In addition, just about everyone wants to learn how to be less frustrated and more satisfied with life. You probably notice that when you are dissatisfied, you often become insecure, judgmental, and sometimes even irritable with others. This book's mission and solution to this common syndrome of dissatisfaction is to help you find your truth and work toward greatness—thereby decreasing frustrations and regrets, fostering greater happiness in your life, and enhancing the lives of those around you as well.

Good luck with your unique and empowering coaching journey! Enjoy the following Inspiration, one of which is in every chapter along with exercises and blogging opportunities. I trust that the former will give you a burst of energy to accomplish the possible, and that the latter will offer you practical ways to reach your goals.

DR. JOE'S INSPIRATION

"Only a courageous person dares to inquire whether they are actually reaching their goals and dreams."

PART I

DECIDING WHETHER TO FIRE YOUR THERAPIST

CHAPTER 1

Why Therapy Might
Not Be Working

It's really not that complicated. Most people want a better and more meaningful life. And they want results. Wherever I go, I hear something along the lines of the following when I'm introduced: "Wow, you're a doctor and a coach! I've been looking for a coach but never knew where to turn." More than ever before, people are seeking alternative forms of help. They're not seeking it because they're abnormal or because they have any type of clinical mental malady. Instead, they want fresh and effective guidance about everything from relationships to careers to spiritual issues.

Just about every day, I encounter someone who confirms my belief about this universal and wide-ranging need for practical life guidance. For instance, I'm in a cab and the driver reveals he is an unemployed Ph.D. in chemistry wishing he had a great career; I'm on an airplane speaking to an executive who is frustrated that he is getting mediocre results in both his marriage and at work; I'm buying a shirt and the salesperson expresses frustration not only because she is not using her master's degree but also because she longs for a spiritual connection to give her life more meaning.

In short, you, like most people, want something more. You don't want someone to tell you what to do per se, but someone to facilitate the design of your master plan and then help you make choices and implement changes. As much as you might like to do all this on your own, you can benefit from a coach, mentor, teacher, or adviser who both motivates you and serves as an accountability figure. This relationship helps you maintain your progress.

We are entering a groundbreaking era of coaching and other change modalities. In the past, coaching tended to be defined narrowly. It was primarily a vehicle for people having trouble with jobs or hoping to enhance sports performance. In recent years, however, the concept of a life coach or an executive coach has emerged and become something of a trend. We're seeing more and more people turn to coaches to help them with a wide range of issues. Coaching methods are expanding and becoming more sophisticated in response. Coaches are learning how to help people achieve peak performance, raise confidence, define the next phase of their career, manage money better, improve their relationships, make more friends, manage their weight and achieve wellness, date more effectively, manage bad habits and even addictions, develop their religious or spiritual sides, design retirement, or search for a more meaningful existence.

Kayla is a good example of someone who probably would have gone it alone in the past, but today recognizes the value of coaching. A junior at an excellent midwestern college, Kayla was feeling pressure from both her school adviser and her parents to choose a major. Kayla was open to this, but had no idea what she truly wanted to choose. To help her select a major, she engaged the services of a coach who was recommended by one of her roommates. The coach encouraged her to begin thinking about what she truly was interested in studying. He provided her with different scenarios to consider; he helped her organize her thinking about different majors and career possibilities. By asking Kayla questions and helping her understand what her responses implied, they were able to narrow the possibilities to three. Of these she finally selected the one she truly wanted: sociology.

Why couldn't Kayla figure this out for herself? This is an important question. The answer is that people are often socialized by their culture, parents, and peers to stop paying attention to what they really want. So a coach will often sift through this interference from others and free the client to discover her true desires. By providing Kayla with a process to analyze her options and by offering objective counsel about those options, the coach was able to help Kayla make a decision.

People like Kayla are normal. Their lives are a work in progress, a work that can be changed in accordance with their hopes and dreams. There is a reason why coaching has been embraced by athletes and the corporate world. Now the public at large can capitalize on coaching techniques and tools to improve just about every aspect of their lives.

Coaching Meets an Emerging Need

The world is smaller: globalization is the rage, whether we like it or not. Due to ever-expanding technologies such as the Internet, overnight global mail, world cell phones, and video conferencing, geographic distance does not seem to matter anymore. Everybody wants a piece of the pie. Resources are scarce. Competition is fierce. Success is harder to come by. The American Dream or what I call the World Dream is harder to attain. There is tremendous concern over terrorism and destruction of the environment. Whether a newly graduating college student, a thirtysomething unhappy with his career choice, or a senior citizen embarking on retirement, most people are hungry for help. Their uncertainty, anxiety, or ambition prompts them to seek assistance.

Normal people, however, often are unsure about where to seek help. Some are willing to try therapy but discover that after a while, it's not meeting their needs, for they don't have a symptom of mental illness for which traditional therapy is equipped to handle. Or they take an effective medication for an isolated mental health symptom, are now symptom-free, and now want coaching to address their life plan. Others avoid therapy completely because of the attached stigma that seeking help is only for those with mental illness. For many years, friends and family would often react to the news of someone being in therapy with a comment such as "What, are you crazy?" Ironically, insurance companies who sometimes pay for mental health services will often turn someone down for a health care or disability plan if they have a "mental health history."

The fact is that Freud and his later disciples would see a normal person working toward life-optimizing goals during one session and then would see an individual with severe mental illness during the next session. I don't believe this "mixed" approach is viable. Different skills and services are needed for normal people versus those with serious mental illness. Unfortunately, many people aren't aware of this distinction. As a result, they are often disappointed with the results of therapy and uncertain if coaching is right for them.

Noah was very bright and in his early thirties. He was also very shy, which made him uneasy when meeting women and dating. He enlisted the help of a therapist, who diagnosed him as having a low-grade depression. In the sessions Noah was asked to discuss his feelings of depression, but Noah said he wasn't depressed and that he was simply shy. The therapist disagreed. Still, Noah continued with the therapy, assuming his therapist would be able to find a way to free him from his debilitating shyness and help him achieve his goal of dating. The therapist, however, was not focused on this goal, at least not as an end in and of itself. He wanted to help Noah dig down deeper and discover the root causes of his shyness. And so Noah and his therapist spent ten sessions digging, and though Noah found the process enlightening and believed the therapist was smart and sincere, he wasn't any closer to his goal of having an easier time relating to women. While he found it interesting to explore the somewhat strained relationship he had with his mother while growing up, this exploration didn't suddenly release him from his shyness. Finally, Noah had enough and stopped going to the therapist.

Two months later, Noah began seeing a coach who specialized in dating issues. The coach helped raise Noah's confidence by referring him to a public speaking course. As his confidence grew at speaking, the coach began to work on his dating skills. He asked Noah to concentrate on meeting women in grocery stores, the gym, and on the Internet and asking them to coffee or a meal. This actually went well and Noah found he had at least one date every weekend. It was a very practical, methodical approach, and it was exactly what Noah needed to overcome his shyness and start meeting women.

Of course, it's not always this simple. Coaching clients can have complex problems that require intervention in many different areas of their lives, and it can take time to achieve their goals. Nonetheless, it's a viable option for normal people, one that has become a highly effective, sophisticated discipline. To understand how this is so, we first need to place normal on a continuum and look at who on that continuum will benefit from coaching.

Coaching Is for Normal People

Please forgive my use of the term "normal." It is a handy word to describe people who don't have serious mental illness, but it is also subject to misinterpretation. All people have issues in their lives that cause discomfort or frustration. At certain points these issues may cause them to feel or act in ways that result in some decrease in normal functioning. They may avoid a certain person; they may lose a job because of their anxiety; they may feel disconnected from others; or they may feel empty inside. During these periods, "normal" may be the last word that comes to mind when describing these individuals. Nonetheless, these people are able to function at a relatively high level throughout their lives. Everybody has down moods and periodic losses. A normal person is usually able to keep going in the face of these losses, frustrations, mild symptoms, and desire for life optimization. They consistently utilize coping skills that prevent repeated lapses into catatonia, a manic rampage, unemployment, or social isolation.

Let's place "normal" on a continuum with mental illness:

Mental Illness	←→	NORMAL	→	Outcomes/Self-actualization
(Therapy & Meds)		(Coaching)		(Goals & Change Attained)
Symptomatic		*Symptom-free or Asymptomatic with Treatment*		

Within this continuum, coaching is useful for the normal group. If you're already fully self-actualized, you probably don't need coaching or therapy. But for many, self-actualization comes out of coaching. If you have symptoms of a mental illness, you frequently require medication and sometimes require therapy as well. If you have ambitious goals you want to achieve in life, it will be important for you to eventually utilize coaching.

Now, of course, many people can move between two of the points on the continuum. For instance, you may begin with a depression and seek medication. When you respond to medication and become asymptomatic, you fall in the normal range and often begin coaching at that point. With the help of medication you function well in the normal range, and with the simultaneous use of coaching you can work toward behavioral change and self-actualization.

When a person begins to work on himself or herself, therapy is often what is utilized because of the large numbers of therapists as compared to coaches. At first, in therapy, talking about feelings is experienced as helpful, and a working through of the past (making peace with family disappointments) is useful. As is frequently the case, as time proceeds, therapy is often no longer useful to many normal people because they begin to need to work on their vision of their future life and goals, and this usually does not get addressed well in therapy, as it does in coaching. Now let's take a more focused look at who can benefit from therapy versus coaching.

Therapy or medication is good for symptoms of mental illness such as depression or anxiety. Cognitive behavioral therapy (CBT), a form of therapy, helps people examine their thoughts and sometimes changes the way they think and feel. CBT aims to lessen symptoms of mental illness. Therapy is also appropriate when people simply want to talk about a significant issue bothering them or causing symptoms.

In other words, when people require a clinical and empathetic ear, therapy is useful. Therapy also is used for significant symptoms of mental illness, and it is useful for people to discuss their past in detail to make peace with their history to whatever extent possible.

Coaching, on the other hand, facilitates working toward one's vision of his or her life and goals; coaching helps effect change and transforms lives. It also is useful for those who want to achieve specific outcomes in some area or areas of their life. Coaching is not mainly about symptoms of mental illness that cause dysfunction. Instead, it focuses on achieving a range of positive objectives, such as doing better in a career, improving relationships, or becoming a more spiritual person. The coaching process may involve some discussion of feelings, but the intent of the discussion is to set the client free to achieve objectives. Unlike therapists, coaches don't confine themselves to one role. Instead, they can help create action plans, offer options, and measure progress toward objectives. They are often hands-on with goal implementation. The coaching process is dedicated to achieving personal or organizational greatness.

Another interesting difference between therapists and coaches involves terminology. Therapists, as do physicians, usually refer to clients as *patients*. This makes sense in that the patients are seen to have disorders and diseases. In contrast, coaches see their clients as *customers* who have come to utilize their services as coaches. For this reason, I call the people who come to see me *clients*. Coaching also tends to follow the lead of the client, while therapy tends to be therapist-driven. For example, the history of providing therapy and analysis included the therapist telling the patient why they were doing things and thinking in certain ways.

I've created the two following lists that spell out the specific problems or indications for which either coaching or therapy is appropriate. Determine which list seems better suited for the issues or goals you're facing:

Frequent Indications for Therapy and/or Medication (Note issues and problems)

- Negative thoughts
- Intensity of emotional symptoms causing dysfunction
- Anxiety
- Depression
- Attention deficit disorder
- Schizophrenia
- Bipolar disorder
- Severe eating disorder
- Severe grief
- Severe addiction (or refuses recovery from or reduction of addictive behavior)
- Shame (feeling inferior to others)

Frequent Indications for Coaching (Note goals)

- Get unstuck
- Achieve vision of life in some or all spheres
- Accomplish career ambitions
- Address performance issues or goals
- Work toward empowerment goals
- Date better
- Enrich significant relationship
- Build resilience
- Manage mild addictions or bad habits (procrastination, sloppiness)
- Improve nutritional habits
- Work toward greater wellness
- Accomplish greater sports performance

- Optimize body image
- Raise self-confidence
- Improve financial management
- Raise school performance
- Increase energy and stamina
- Manage severe addictions while compliant with recovery

Looking at these two lists, you may still find yourself in a quandary about whether you require therapy or coaching. You may be suffering from anxiety, yet you also want to get unstuck and achieve goals and vision. It's possible that you could benefit from medication as well as coaching. The odds are, however, that once treated, you fall within the normal range of the continuum, so that even if you're somewhere between mental illness and normal, coaching would be a good choice. Remember that coaching is compatible with medication if you are completely or almost symptom-free.

If you're still unsure if coaching or therapy is better for you, or if you should fire your therapist and switch to a coach, consider the specific benefits people report achieving from being coached:

Potential Gains from Coaching (Outcomes)

- Achieved vision and goals
- Improved career performance and satisfaction
- Stronger relationships
- More effective dating
- Greater resilience when stressed
- Improved nutrition
- Better body image
- Weight management
- More friends/better friendships
- Improved family relationships
- More community involvement/volunteering
- Working out regularly and more effectively
- More involvement in spirituality or organized religion

- More fun
- Better home environment created
- Improved leadership qualities
- More purpose
- Improved task and time management
- Greater happiness and satisfaction
- More and better sex
- Empowerment
- Bad habits managed
- Better management of substance use and other addictions (person is in good control or in recovery)
- Greater self-confidence
- Achieved financial goals and improved money management
- Optimized school performance
- Increased energy and stamina
- Athletic prowess
- Optimized wellness
- Life more in balance

I suspect that one or more of the gains found in the outcomes listed above are high on your priority list. If so, coaching may be your better option.

Here's another way to make the determination between therapy and coaching. Coaching is for normal people, and though the boundaries of normality can become a bit hazy, you can determine if you fall roughly within its boundaries by using the following checklist:

Normality Checklist

- ☐ Are generally content with life, even if you have goals yet to accomplish
- ☐ Cope well with some of the problems you encounter
- ☐ Function effectively in many (if not all) areas of your life
- ☐ Have not been diagnosed with a specific mental disorder (or it's in remission)

☐ Have a grip on the reality of your situation (even if you're not handling it effectively)

☐ Are accomplished at some aspects of your life

☐ Have some productive, fulfilling relationships

☐ Have no severe addictions to drugs or alcohol (or in recovery)

☐ Find satisfaction and meaning in at least some activities

Here's another way to look at normality. The following are common situations people face. After each situation, I'll suggest whether coaching or therapy is called for. Use these "if-then" scenarios to evaluate if therapy or coaching would be better for you:

If-Then Scenarios

If I believe a lot of what I do for a living isn't particularly meaningful, *then* I need to see a coach.

If I sit in my room all day and have trouble even making a phone call, let alone holding a job or going out with friends, *then* I need to see a therapist.

If I haven't had a date in more than a year and am unable to form a romantic relationship, *then* I need to see a coach.

If I can't go to the store without having a panic attack, *then* I need to see a therapist or a psychiatrist.

If I have adopted a series of ritual behaviors such as washing my hands fifty times a day or checking locks obsessively that prevent me from enjoying even routine activities, *then* I need to see a therapist or a psychiatrist.

If I am neurotic about catching certain diseases and am often anxious when facing stressful situations, *then* I need to see a therapist.

If I believe everyone is out to get me and suspect people are spying on me, *then* I need to see a therapist or a psychiatrist.

If I find myself struggling to find a sense of purpose, *then* I need to see a coach.

If I find myself hurting myself in some way or have suicidal thoughts, *then* I need to see a therapist.

If I'm pessimistic about my chances for meaningful relationships and convinced that I'm never going to be successful in my career, *then* I need to see a coach.

How You Know You Are Ready for Coaching

You are talked out. You have talked to friends, relatives, and even therapists. You find you are searching for something or are just not satisfied, but just talking about it does not help you feel better any more. You know you are headed somewhere but you need some sort of facilitator to guide you or at last accompany you down the path. You want to make your own decisions, but it would be useful to have someone understand you and help present alternative choices, to work with someone who has a method to guide you in planning the next phase of your life and career. Everyone you know seems to just listen or tell you advice that you don't find useful. Deep inside, you realize it is time to work with a coach, someone who understands that your life is a work in progress and that you are ready to work hard at it again.

But I'm getting ahead of myself. Let's begin by reading the following Inspiration and then completing the following exercise, The Ocean Yell. You'll also see that I've included an example of how a client completed this exercise. In addition, you'll find this individual's sample blog, designed to encourage you to write your thoughts in a blog online or in a journal, about the topics discussed in this chapter and how they relate to you.

DR. JOE'S INSPIRATION

"Coaching unlocks your deepest wishes by raising the possibility and probability that buried truth can be transformed into vibrant reality."

Full Life Exercise

The Ocean Yell

If I were to yell on an empty beach with the waves breaking (no one else can overhear) . . . what do I want in my life that is not there now, what would I yell out in each sphere?

Sphere	I would yell the following: "I want . . . "
Self	
Work	
Love	
Family	
Body	
Friends	
Community	
Spirit	
Money	
Fun	
Home	

SUSAN'S RESPONSE

Sphere	I would yell the following: "I want . . ."
Self	I want to be confident!
Work	I want a career I love!
Love	I want a great boyfriend and eventual husband!
Family	I want to get along with my father!
Body	I want to lose twenty-five pounds!
Friends	I want a few more close friends!

(continued)

Sphere	I would yell the following: "I want . . ."
Community	I want to volunteer somewhere!
Spirit	I want to believe in something bigger than every-thing!
Money	I want more money so I won't have to worry!
Fun	I want to have more fun!
Home	I want to have a home I love!

SUSAN'S BLOG

I am ready for coaching. I want to get my life in shape. Specifically, I want to address my issues and work toward things I really want. I want to get less anxious and stop getting so irritated with others. This seems unnecessary and unhelpful to me. I want to make my current job more interesting so I don't get bored. I want to have a great relationship someday. I want to accept my parents' divorce so I can get on with my life. I need to manage my occasional binging and purging. I need to make new friends. I want to be part of a group of friends or at least take part in more group activities. I want to explore other faiths and forms of spirituality. I want to save more money and cut spending on clothes. I want to enjoy life more. I would like a bigger apartment soon.

I am looking forward to working with my coach.

CHAPTER 2

What to Expect from Coaching

Coaching, like therapy, varies based on the professional you see and his or her approach. Going to a Freudian analyst five days per week is very different from weekly sessions with a social worker trained in a family systems model. Working with a career coach is quite different from working with one who is more spiritually oriented.

In other words, coaching is a broad concept, and your experience with a coach may not be the same as someone else's. Nonetheless, certain commonalities exist no matter what type of coach you have, and it's important for you to understand what you're likely to encounter. It's especially important to understand what you should get out of a coaching experience; this provides you with a barometer to gauge whether your coach is effective.

Let's start out by defining a coaching experience in contrast to a therapy experience so the differences are clear.

Less Stigma with Coaching

Let's say that at some time in the past ten years or so, you decided you needed to see a therapist. Here is what probably took place. Upon meeting the counselor or therapist or after a series of sessions, you were told you had a disorder called such and such. Once labeled, you felt the stigma of being diagnosed with mental illness. You may have started therapy with the hope of feeling happier, better able to deal with a problematic situation, or possessing a stronger sense of purpose, but instead you are told you have a disorder. Even if the sessions with the therapist are helpful in grasping why you have symptoms of the alleged disorder, after a while you often feel as if you're not getting anywhere. There's a lot of talk but no action or movement toward solutions. You have goals you hoped therapy would help you achieve, and instead you're not experiencing these outcomes. There's no plan, no time frame for taking action, no way to measure your progress. If you're normal, the process can be both stigmatizing and frustrating. Every time you bring up your eagerness for progress your therapist interprets your wanting progress as just another of your problems. The therapist reminds you that it is the process that matters, not the goals.

Nonetheless, many people go into therapy believing that if they can deal effectively with their psychological issues, they can free themselves to deal effectively with more practical goals. It is enticing logic that has some long-term validity, but for people who fall within the normal range and have issues they want and need to handle now, therapy can be a mistake.

Laura, for instance, had come up with a plan to start her own knitting supply business. However, she lacked the confidence to go ahead with her business plan because she heard her mother's voice in her head telling her that she was a failure and was always going to be a failure. She engaged the services of a therapist and hoped that the process would free her to be successful at the business venture. Instead, the therapy concentrated on Laura's alleged "low self-esteem" and the causes of it. Laura had a controlling, highly successful father, and the therapist spent a lot of time talking to Laura about her father and their relationship. No doubt this was an issue in Laura's life. Dealing with this issue, however, wasn't having any impact on Laura's desire to muster the inner strength to pursue her business dream. The therapist, for instance, barely addressed why Laura didn't have confidence, since she seemed to have the skills, knowledge, and resources necessary to launch her new business. Nonetheless, Laura persevered with the therapy for two years. It was almost as if the therapy gave her an excuse not to start her knitting supply business, that she could postpone doing what she feared as long as she was in therapy. Finally, though, Laura's dream of being on her own overpowered her fear, and she told the therapist she was frustrated and wasn't going to be coming back.

Contrast this with the coaching process. In coaching, you would first perform a detailed inquiry into your life regarding what is going well and what is not going well. You are affirmed and honored by the coach for taking responsibility for your life design. You spend some time exploring things such as your strengths and weaknesses, values, mission, and purpose—as well as your vision of your future. You then establish your priority goals and begin working toward what I call next-step goals (to reach your priority goals). You are encouraged by your coach to set timelines to reach your priority goals. Goal completion is emphasized by your coach. You are constantly acknowledged for accomplishing your goals and moving into your desired future. There is no mention of disorder, disease, and problems unless it relates to difficulty achieving one of your goals. If you tell your coach you are eager to move a little faster, your coach asks, "How fast?"

When Laura was trying to decide what to do next, she read an article about career coaches and called up one of the coaches interviewed in the article, since he specialized in business advice. They began working together, and the coach assigned several homework assignments for Laura to manage her negative thoughts, as well as having her take vitamins and work out regularly, since she seemed fatigued even though she had no medical problems. The coach also began to assign her business planning tasks, culminating in a completed business plan. Energized and much more positive about herself than in the past, Laura presented the business plan to the Small Business Administration and was approved for a business start-up loan. Six months after starting coaching, Laura was in a storefront rental property and readying her knitting supply store for business.

What Should a Coach Provide?

What are your expectations of a coach and the process? Some people want a coach to take charge of their lives, tell them exactly what to do, and solve their problems in a short time. They see a coach as the opposite of a therapist, as someone who will not just sit and listen and ask questions but as a kind of personal facilitator and champion.

To assess your own expectations, take the following true/false quiz:

1. The best coach is one who can stop me from doing what I want and explain what I should be doing.
   True
   False
2. A coach who says "I don't know" is not the coach for me.
   True
   False
3. The best coaches usually have no training in psychology.
   True
   False
4. I will get the best results from a coach who is constantly pushing and prodding me to do better.
   True
   False

5. Coaches come in many different varieties, and I should choose the one whose experience and expertise best match my life goals.

True

False

6. A coach should be able to help me make progress on addressing my issues or goals within one month of starting to see him.

True

False

7. I expect a coach to help me with short-term as well as long-term life challenges, no matter what they might be.

True

False

Answers

1. **False.** Coaches don't tell their clients what not to do ... or what to do, for that matter. They are facilitators, cheerleaders, planners, and monitors, but they are not gurus dispensing some great truth.

2. **False.** Coaches are less likely than therapists to presume more knowledge than they possess. They are more likely to admit lack of knowledge and demonstrate a willingness to refer clients to people who know what they don't.

3. **False.** Some coaches come from the psychological arena and some do not. Most are attracted to the coaching field because it allows them to provide normal people with more immediate, results-producing assistance.

4. **False.** While coaches can motivate and inspire their clients to improve, some of the most effective can be the opposite of the stereotypical gruff-and-tough football coach. People need to find the coach whose personality is right for them.

5. **True.** One of the great things about coaching is that the field encompasses all types of knowledge, expertise, and

experience. Therefore you should be selective in choosing a coach, looking for one who has specific areas of training and skills that dovetail with your issues.

6. **False.** While coaching usually does produce results faster than therapy, the time frames vary considerably. Your coach should help you figure out an ideal time frame for taking certain actions and achieving certain goals, but you should not equate solutions for specific problems with a definite period of time—saying that couple issues take one month to cure, for instance.

7. **True.** While coaches are great at zeroing in on issues and helping you deal with them sooner rather than later, they also are concerned about long-range plans. In this way, they avoid providing clients with emotional Band-Aids.

Clearly, you're going to be disappointed if this quiz reflects inaccurate expectations. Coaching doesn't work overnight, and every coach is not ideal for every client. Like any process, coaching takes time and effort on your part for it to work. At the same time, you should have more "practical" expectations of it than therapy. You have every right to believe that it will help you achieve specific goals. And you also should expect to be a much more active participant in the process than in therapy. Rather than a boss, your coach will be a facilitator for you to design and implement the next phase of your life.

Dena had been in therapy for ten years. She had much greater self-understanding and had made peace with her family of origin's strengths and weaknesses. Now she decided to work with a coach to achieve a more meaningful life. She wasn't sure what this life would look like, yet she was excited to begin this work with a coach.

The following is a list of ten things you can expect to receive from any coach:

1. A warm, affirming response
2. An inquiry into what is going well and what is not going well in all aspects of your life

3. Exploration of values, mission, and purpose
4. Visioning exercises to establish what you want your life to look like
5. Assistance in formulating specific priority goals to achieve your vision
6. Help creating a plan to achieve incremental steps toward the priority goals
7. Tools for managing addictions, bad habits, and bad attitudes
8. Working toward priority goals one incremental step at a time
9. Measurement and acknowledgment of outcome achievement
10. Follow-up plan in place to support long-term maintenance and success

These ten points are the least you can expect from a coach. They characterize the results orientation of the process as well as the support, advice, and accountability built into it. Use these expectations as a checklist to monitor how the coaching process is going. If your coach is falling short in one or more areas, talk to him or her about it. Unlike many therapists, your coach should be amenable to adjusting the approach to help you meet your goals.

Seeking Greatness Rather than What's Wrong

Coaching is revolutionary in that it is client-centric. This means that it focuses on what clients want rather than on judgment and interpretation, the mainstays of therapy. When therapists judge their patients, they also pathologize them, making them feel as if they have a serious and possibly long-term condition. When they interpret what is wrong, the process often becomes bogged down in the past, in assumption and judgment—rather than looking toward the future and the client's ambitions.

As you probably understand at this point, coaching takes a very different view of customers and sees them as clients. Coaches don't assume that people have something wrong with them when they enter their offices. In fact, they assume that something is right; otherwise they wouldn't have the wherewithal to optimize their lives and careers. Wanting to design a life-optimization plan is a positive action and fascinating journey, and coaches affirm people who are eager to embark on this life-changing task.

Coaching's ultimate goal is highly ambitious—it is about greatness. This is true whether it's an individual wanting to lead a more meaningful life or an organization wanting to help key people perform at the highest possible level. It is vital that individuals and organizations begin to get concerned about being the best they can be through creativity, hard work, values, and productivity goals. The individual goal may be greater satisfaction with life and even increased longevity and wellness. The organizational goal may be to become a more profitable, productive, and ethical organization.

Instead of just getting by, coaching opens the door to peak performance for all of us. What does that look like? How can each of us be better? How can each of us work toward being the best we can be in any area of life? Throughout history, the concept of being your best was primarily a religious notion. In recent history, however, a shift has occurred: now it is increasingly taken for granted that we each need to think about our individual purpose and goals and work toward personal greatness. Coaching dovetails with this modern mind-set of striving for betterment for self and others.

In the early days of therapy, the talking cure was hailed as a breakthrough, highly effective technique. To this day, people swear by their therapists and how their talking sessions are cathartic and insightful. That's because talking does help some people connect and feel better. It helps them be "seen" and feel less alone, less shamed, and less fearful.

Coaching, too, employs the talking cure, but it is only one of hundreds of techniques utilized by your coach. Coaching is an outcome-oriented, multi-modality, and multipronged approach.

In coaching, there is so much to get done that it is impossible to just talk! You may have goals that range from becoming more spiritual to finding a new career to becoming a more active participant in a community. As a result, a coach may need to work with you on creating a career strategy. He may recommend meditation or volunteering as part of your coaching goals. Recognize that coaching makes numerous options available to you. Be open to the possibilities your coach suggests, even if they are unconventional. A good coach has a varied palette to work with, and you should be ready to take advantage of it.

Coaching as a Holistic Discipline

Just because you're normal doesn't mean you're a simple organism. The coaching perspective is that normal people are enormously complex. In fact, the only way to navigate and facilitate a person's coaching is to see how the person is functioning in all aspects of life. Only then can a coach come up with a comprehensive plan that addresses these key areas. For example, a person's *self* might be addressed by working on issues related to confidence, but a person's *body* might be addressed with a commitment to go to the neighborhood gym three times a week.

What I call multidimensional coaching is the wave of the future—it is the logical evolution of all the different healing movements that have emerged in recent years. Consumerist movements that drive change in other fields have begun to affect the self-improvement fields as well. People feel more empowered than ever before to make specific treatment suggestions. While therapists may not always be amenable to these suggestions, coaches are responsive to them. More than that, they invite their clients to participate as partners in the process. This interaction produces coaching plans that range far and wide, and they are as likely to focus on dating or parenting or religious issues as on traditional matters of the self.

Keep in mind that people seek out coaches for many reasons— because they are in an existential crisis, long for greater human connection, have unmet desires, are anxious, or are suffering from low self-esteem. These are normal people who are hurting or searching or both. Or they are extremely talented people seeking higher and higher functioning in life and work. In the past, they may have simply suffered or searched in silence. Today, they feel emboldened to ask coaches for help or accountability. Coaches are responding with a much more holistic approach than existed even a few years ago. They are coaching people in terms of multiple dimensions rather than simply one or two areas.

A coach's multidimensional perspective is an outgrowth of all the amazing developments in society—the Internet, the spirituality movement, the notion of work as a calling, the breakthroughs in physical wellness. As everyone becomes more aware of the possibilities for living a full life, they will drive the coaching process in a variety of fresh directions. While coaches should not be expected to be experts in every area from yoga to Internet businesses, they should be aware of all these areas and be able to refer their clients to experts when necessary. In this way, the self-imposed limits of traditional therapy are removed from coaching. It may be that one person's path to a more meaningful life is through outdoor survival experiences. Another person may find fresh purpose by turning her love of cooking into a career as a chef and by deciding to adopt a child. The possibilities are endless, and good coaches don't rule out any of these possibilities.

Neither should you limit your options as the coaching client. Just as therapists must stop viewing the people they're helping as "sick," "damaged," or "flawed" and start seeing them as quirky, fascinating, and strong people, you, too, need to adopt this latter perspective about yourself. Recognize that you may not need ten years of intensive self-based talk therapy, but instead can make leaps in personal growth through meditation, coaching, joining community groups, or pursuing all sorts of other nontraditional healing alternatives. By changing your perspective on what self-improvement is, you free yourself from self-imposed limits of what you can accomplish. It is a coach's job to encourage you in this unlimited and creative approach to changing your life, and to provide you with the tools, referrals, and talk that will make these changes feasible.

Beyond the Talking Cure: Give People the Exercises to Work On between Sessions

In traditional therapy, progress is generally made within scheduled sessions with the therapist. Typically, the therapist controls the process and determines how much progress to make and how quickly. Though some therapists may assign patients some homework, relatively little is accomplished outside of the office.

Today a slew of coaching exercises can help you progress on your own between sessions. Our coaching exercises at Full Life are related to the many dimensions of life just discussed, and they include many creative homework assignments that ask you to pursue investigations—such as inquiries to determine what is going well and what is not going well and what you want to concentrate on in your life. The priority goals fall into eleven diverse areas we call the Spheres of Life. The exercises at the end of each chapter in this book are examples of coaching homework.

For now, though, I'd like to give you a few descriptions of some of our core coaching exercises:

- *Life Investigation:* a tool that will guide you in an inquiry into how you are functioning in each of the eleven dimensions we call spheres. This will establish your current strengths and weaknesses. You can find it at the end of chapter 8.
- *Vision Picture:* a process that helps you paint with words and pictures and therefore describe what your life will look like in all eleven spheres in the future. This exercise helps you to look beyond and break out of your current situation and mind-set. What's amazing about this exercise is that much of it will come true at a later date in your life.

- *Achilles Plan:* goal-setting techniques to help you establish an effective approach to bring your vision into reality and focus over time by setting next-step goals to eventually achieve your priority goals. You will come across it near the end of chapter 12.

Later we'll address these exercises in greater detail and you'll be able to apply them to your life. At this point, though, I just want you to think about how they help define the coaching process and differentiate it from the traditional therapeutic one.

When Coaching and Another Modality Are Both Necessary

Most coaches aren't psychiatrists. Most don't have any training as psychologists or social workers. And most therapists and psychiatrists are not coaches. So it is possible that a client might have started with therapy, and then decided to use career coaching while he remained in therapy. For example, Steven first went to therapy because of low self-confidence and heightened anxiety. In therapy he learned ways of managing his anxiety, and his confidence rose. Feeling better allowed Steven to find a career coach. He was not ready to leave therapy, so he did therapy and coaching simultaneously. This is fine if the two modalities don't overlap in agendas. If therapy addressed the symptoms of anxiety and coaching targeted career planning, there was a clear reason to be in both modalities for Steven. In fact, he needed a coach to work with him and help him create a structured, step-by-step plan to become a high school history teacher. Steven needed a coach who would help him figure out the practical issues involved in obtaining a degree, choosing a school, and finding a job. Coaching lowered Steven's risk, at least in his own mind, because he had someone to turn to when he became anxious about his decision. Talking to a coach and referring to a plan helped Steven calm down and recognize that he was pursuing a logical and appropriate goal in the best way possible.

A coach may do a terrific job of helping someone work toward a specific goal, but if a significant issue isn't addressed, an unhelpful behavior will often resurface and sabotage the client's progress in coaching. For example, Ben was unhappy with how his career in advertising was progressing. Though he had done relatively well as an account executive at a major ad agency, he wasn't particularly satisfied by the work. For a number of years he had thought about going back to school and obtaining a doctorate in anthropology; he had completed a number of courses toward that degree years ago but had to drop out and get a job because of financial problems. As we worked on a plan to help Ben transition to this new career, it became apparent that he had a drinking problem. In fact, his drinking was so frequent and severe that it became clear he needed to address it before anything else. One of his parents was an alcoholic, and unless Ben worked on managing his drinking, it would sabotage any other plans he made. During a coaching session, we agreed that he should enter a rehabilitation facility, work with a trained addictions therapist there, and then continue the coaching when his drinking was being successfully managed. Today Ben is back in coaching and also attends Alcoholics Anonymous (AA) meetings regularly and works with an AA sponsor as well on the 12 steps. He has applied to and been accepted in an anthropology doctoral program. Ben continues to set his alcohol recovery goals with his coach as well as his sponsor. He is also using his coach to help him increase his school performance in the doctoral program.

Therefore, a good coach knows when to add another facilitator to the client's plan. In Ben's case he temporarily had to go to a rehabilitation facility and then resume coaching and AA. Usually most issues can be addressed directly by a competent coach. But a good coach also knows when it is time to give specialty referrals to the client, such as the rehab facility and the sponsor.

So coaching can go on with different forms of specialty coaching, therapy, and self-help groups. Sometimes people are in therapy and they come to work on career coaching because their careers did not improve with therapy alone, but they still found the therapy valuable. It is less common that a client adds therapy to coaching. It is my experience that due to the comprehensiveness of coaching, many areas of life are addressed.

I do see 12-step groups such as Alcoholics Anonymous, Marijuana Anonymous, Narcotics Anonymous, and Gamblers Anonymous as highly compatible with coaching. Spiritual advisers and men's or women's groups seem very compatible as well. If both client and coach are comfortable with the add-on of a specialty coach or activity, it is probably okay.

Rowan came to coaching to improve his job performance. He was CEO and founder of a contracting group that specialized in commercial building. He was concerned that his company was losing some of its best customers due to complaints about his company's service. Rowan knew that a lot of the problems could be traced to him. During the third session, Rowan admitted that he had a serious marijuana problem causing a lot of dysfunction in his life—especially decreased motivation. He said he was using daily and sometimes as frequently as twice a day. Rowan agreed to slowly stop using marijuana. He made up a schedule and successfully stopped using. He attended Marijuana Anonymous (MA) and worked closely with a sponsor. Rowan continued to do very well in coaching. He did have one brief relapse with marijuana, but he was successful at getting back on track with the help of his MA sponsor and his coach. Today Rowan and his company have doubled their revenues and Rowan continues to be free of his marijuana problem.

Now that you have a better sense of what coaching does and does not involve, think about what you would like to get out of the process. Is it finding a true calling? Is it feeling a connection with something larger than you? Is it meeting someone with whom you can share your life? Is it making a better relationship with a spouse or significant other?

Troubleshooting

Clients work very hard with their coach in trying to reach desired goals and outcomes. This section covers issues that sometimes arise and have to be negotiated by both client and coach to achieve outcomes. Some of the common issues are covered below.

What to do if your coach seems unable to help you in some spheres

All coaches have limitations (believe it or not!). You may need help in a sphere where the coach lacks interest or training. For example, Fatima was getting more and more interested in developing and exploring her spirituality. Her coach was an atheist who really couldn't relate to Fatima's interest. The solution Fatima and her coach came up with was for her to work with a spiritual adviser from her faith of interest.

What to do if you are seeing a specialty coach and you have goals in the other ten spheres

If you are seeing a specialty coach at first and then you get interested in working on optimizing your life in all spheres, you need to find another coach who would be comfortable working with you as you continue with the specialty coach. You would need agreement that the new coach would not duplicate the areas you are already making progress on with the specialty coach.

Paris was working for six months with a dating coach. She had made a lot of progress and was regularly going on dates. Then she became interested in working with a coach on the ten other spheres. A friend referred her to a coach with more generalized expertise, and she met with her for an initial session. She asked the coach if she would be comfortable if Paris continued to work with the dating coach. The coach said that she would not be comfortable but referred Paris to a colleague who she thought would be fine with it. Paris liked the person she was referred to, and she continued to work with her dating coach. The combination of coaches allowed her to make more progress in all spheres.

How long should achieving outcomes take with a coach?

I am asked this question all the time. The time can range from several sessions to many years, depending on how comprehensively the client wants to address the spheres. Some clients come wanting to work on a single sphere, which usually can take as few as six months. Other clients want to work on all eleven spheres and can be in coaching for at least a few years. Entrepreneurial clients building their own businesses from scratch are often in coaching for at least a few years. Some clients believe they live a life closer to greatness when they are in coaching as contrasted with when they are on their own, so they stay with it for years and continue to work toward new goals. The answer is that everyone chooses a different length of time.

Calvin came in because he broke up with his girlfriend and was despairing and not sleeping or eating regularly. He wanted a few sessions to talk about his breakup and see if he could start feeling better and resume his normal routines. Calvin actually spent six months in coaching, two sessions per month. The first sessions helped him get through the grief of breakup, and then he began to talk about what he learned from his former relationship. He resumed his normal sleeping and eating habits. Soon he began to talk about the type of woman he would like to meet and the qualities she would possess. Then he slowly began to date again. At the fifth month, he was dating a very nice woman and he was quite content. At the end of his six months he thanked his coach and went on with his life without coaching. At some point in the future, he might return to coaching to work on something else that comes up, but for now he is doing well.

When you should strike out on your own

I always tell clients that they no longer need to be coached when:

- they have achieved many of their goals and outcomes that originally brought them to coaching;
- it is a time of relatively smooth sailing in their life, not a time of chaos and stress.

Yasmin had come to coaching wanting to define and implement her new business as a personal shopper and style consultant. The first six months were spent on her business plan, and she was very anxious about getting started with the actual business. At the same time, Yasmin continued to talk about her mother in coaching sessions, complaining bitterly that her mother had held her back by always dismissing her talents and ambition. When she told her coach she was going out on her own, her coach noted that she hadn't yet implemented her business plan. The coach also asked her if she really wanted her help in doing this and breaking through her fears about her own self-worth. It was clear to the coach that Yasmin still had issues that were preventing her from implementing her business plan, even though she claimed she wanted to get started on her own. Yasmin immediately acknowledged that she wasn't ready to leave and stayed in coaching for another six months; she simply needed a little nudge from her coach to admit that she still had important priority goals to accomplish.

On the other hand, Jake had come to coaching to start his own barbershop. He had successfully completed a business plan, purchased a space, and decorated the new barbershop. It was now open for one year, and business was better every month. At this time, Jake appropriately decided to stop his coaching because he had accomplished his priority goal: the barbershop. He was proud of his significant accomplishment and knew he could always come back to coaching. Everything was relatively calm in his life, and his confidence was strong. For Jake, it was time to take a healthy break from coaching.

Now read the Inspiration and then complete The No. 1 Priority exercise. Refer to the client's sample completed exercise. Then blog in your journal or online, using the sample blog to guide your efforts.

DR. JOE'S INSPIRATION

*"At long last, normal people can be affirmed for turning
to coaching for life design and planning instead of getting
diagnosed as mentally ill."*

Full Life Exercise

The No. 1 Priority

What is the main thing I am seeking, need to address, or want to work toward?

My No. 1 priority is:

_____

_____

Other priorities include:

_____

_____

STEVEN'S RESPONSE

My No. 1 priority is:
I need to develop a career plan where I will practice my calling and also make a six-figure salary.

Other priorities include:
I want to give back to the community and seek to have a more meaningful life, as this would allow me to feel proud. I want to run a company that produces a good salary but also benefits other people and possibly even benefits communities. I am not sure what my company will do, but I am willing to define my objectives so that I realize my career choice soon. I also want to become more spiritually involved.

STEVEN'S BLOG

I am really excited that I am doing coaching. It is very cool that it has nothing to do with being crazy. I just want to have a great job someday. Is that too much to ask? I want to be proud of my life and be at my best. I am tired of just talking about it. I am going to do it!

CHAPTER 3

Commitment,
Accountability, and
Responsibility

In many patient-therapist relationships, the therapist maintains a neutral, uninvolved persona while the patient absolves himself or herself of all responsibility for the outcome of the therapeutic process. They can spend years together working on issues without anyone making a commitment to a goal or a plan or without anyone being held accountable.

Emma, for instance, was in therapy for ten years. She had a distant father and was sexually abused by a junior high school teacher. Emma and her therapist spent ten years working on healing from the abuse and her feelings about her father. However, she was still working as a receptionist and had no career goals. She was lonely and overweight. Emma also felt a lack of what she called "connection"—she was a lapsed Catholic and felt she had neglected the spiritual side of her life. These were all significant issues, yet the therapist didn't directly address any of them. His training was to dig down and search for root causes, so Emma allowed her therapist to keep digging and didn't require him to show her that she was making progress. The therapist certainly didn't hold Emma accountable for making strides in terms of her career, weight, or spirituality.

In coaching, the situation is much different. In fact, client transformation depends on client and coach mutual commitment *and* client accountability to the coach. This is no different from the coaching process of an Olympic athlete—optimal performance requires total mutual commitment by the athlete and the coach, and then the coach holds the athlete accountable for high performance. The coaching process also requires personal responsibility by the client. This can be a big change for people who have been in therapy and held their therapists responsible for their progress. While the coach facilitates this progress, the client bears the primary responsibility for a positive attitude and the discipline to work toward goals.

Why the Client Leads and the Coach Follows

Following the lead of the client is revolutionary, at least in contrast to a traditional therapy perspective. Despite some therapists' protests to the contrary, most therapists have pathologized, diagnosed, judged, and in effect limited the client's creativity and progress. As discussed in the introduction, even solution-focused therapy focused on problems instead of simply what the client wanted. Coaching reverses the power in the caregiver/care receiver equation. It is up to the client, via the sessions and homework assignments, to develop a voice about what he or she wants life to look like in the future. This sounds easy, but it is not. People often go through life with people telling them what they can and cannot do. It is often frightening or at least challenging, even for the toughest executives, to be given carte blanche to do anything they want for the next phase of their career or family life.

Sandra spent her whole life (all thirty-three years of it) being told what she could and couldn't do. As a child she grew up in the South and was a very studious, overly serious young girl. She was highly disciplined by her parents, and she rarely socialized with peers, but went on to an Ivy League college and was president of the law review in law school. She then went on to land a position at a prestigious law firm specializing in corporate acquisitions. However, at age thirty-three she came to me for coaching, expressing a vague dissatisfaction with her life direction. At first it was very difficult for her to look me in the eye and say what was on her mind. Through the homework exercises, though, she started telling me what was going well in her life and what was not going so well. She began to reveal her dissatisfaction with the legal profession and her loneliness from being single. Sandra admitted both were causing depressive symptoms and that she was worried about herself for the first time. Sandra was one of those people who always looked like a success from the outside. She was a great student who had landed a top job, but she also felt like a fish out of water. Sandra was part of a rural southern black family where few family members had gone to college and no one had gone to a top law school, been hired by a prestigious firm, or achieved the professional success she had. For this reason, she found it extremely challenging to voice what she was seeking. She finally started to discuss her plans to leave the law, become a teacher, and learn how to date well because she wanted a family of her own. Her voice emerged, as did some new and important goals.

I followed Sandra's lead. I listened and encouraged her to talk about and articulate what she really wanted from coaching. If I had taken a traditional therapist's approach, I probably would have wasted a great deal of time exploring areas that might have been of clinical interest to me but of no practical use to Sandra. By giving Sandra permission to let her voice emerge and by allowing her to articulate what she was feeling without judgment or pathologizing her need to reevaluate her career and life,

Sandra was able to state her goals. This would not have happened—or would not have happened as quickly—if I had asked Sandra to follow my lead.

Explode the Myth of Neutrality

Throughout the history of therapy, some therapists have always claimed and still claim that they follow the lead of the client. In most instances, what they are really saying is that they listen to the patient but actually follow the dictates of their training and processes. Similarly, some therapists insist that they practice neutrality, but they are neutral only in a godlike, judgmental sense. When they pathologize normal people with issues, they show a clear bias toward viewing patients as diseased. Neutrality was Freud's concept to protect the client from the therapist's projections onto the client (known as countertransference). But if a therapist is judging or trying to control the client, neutrality is not truly being practiced.

Throughout the history of therapy, minorities were often victims of therapists when, in reality, neutrality was breached. Even though pathologizing has hurt many people in therapy, minorities have been especially injured by judgment stemming from cultural bias. Women, African Americans, gays and lesbians, Hispanics, and many other minorities were often judged and further oppressed by therapists—the very people they turned to for help and true neutrality. That is why, to this day, minorities often avoid therapy, because of the stories passed down to them of abuse and bias.

For example, years ago, before it was popular to have a career alongside men, a woman who wished to choose nontraditional career paths or life paths would most likely be judged by a therapist. For instance, Susan wanted to be a firefighter and also happened to be a lesbian. Years ago, if she had worked with a therapist, it would have been likely that her therapist would have pathologized both her hopes to be a firefighter and the fact that she had a lesbian orientation. This judgment coming from her therapist would have made it impossible for her to thrive in her therapy.

Raymond, a black architect, sought help for confidence issues. He had low self-esteem like so many other people. He wanted to address it because he suffered from anxiety-causing performance issues at the workplace and in his sexual relationship with his wife. He sought therapy, and his therapist told him that part of his problem might be not being as intelligent as other people at his job and that he probably would never fit in. Raymond wisely fired the therapist and decided to look for a new therapist who would address his issues in a helpful and affirming manner.

Biases in therapy continue to this day. Coaching offers all people an opportunity to work on their life design in true neutrality, in an environment of positive regard without judgment and interpretation. When both parties are committed, accountable, and responsible, it is much easier to go forward without prejudices or hidden agendas creeping into the process.

Confront the Fear of the Unknown

Fear of change often sidetracks people in therapy. Fear keeps patients from moving toward goals; from continuing in therapy; and from making needed progress in therapy. The therapist interprets possible reasons for the fears, but clients are often overwhelmed with fear and cannot work past or through the feelings.

Fear also comes up with coaching. At some point in the process, clients freeze. This happens because clients start talking about issues that raise their anxiety levels, or they start exploring feelings they've repressed. Fear of the unknown ties them up in knots. Fear can include concerns of becoming a different person (such as a fat person becoming thin, or a lonely person now adjusting to having someone around), difficulty dealing with a new opportunity (such as a new hobby or a new career), and so on. Ironically, people often fear having their deepest wishes come true. However, too often, people make little progress once they become afraid. Or even worse, they stop working with their coach to avoid the fear. Without an environment of mutual commitment, accountability, and responsibility, it's very difficult for people to continue moving forward with and through their fear.

So fear is just as likely to surface in the coaching process as in therapy, but it's handled differently. Let me describe my experiences. I can see fear emerging in coaching clients, sometimes as early as in our first session together. Early on, most clients are excited to get going and want to talk, do coaching homework, are positive, and believe there is no limit to the change possible. Sooner rather than later, however, the fear strikes. Saying one wants change and actually doing it are two different things. At times, people stop progressing in coaching when this fear sets in—either too much change is attempted or new behaviors are too unfamiliar. The most common signs of this fear emerging are clients saying things such as "I did my homework, but I forgot it." The night before a session they might e-mail me and say, "I am coming but don't expect any homework because I have been too busy." Or they go from being a client who always completes their next-step goals to someone who may take three months to achieve the simplest goal. Less experienced coaches (and therapists) are sometimes naive regarding these resistances and become frustrated when good clients suddenly don't do what they say they want to work toward.

When fear surfaces in this way, effective coaches embrace this emotion as part of the healing and growing process. In fact, I'm convinced this resistance is normal and that I just have to hang in there with the client and wait it out. Just as naturally, the client snaps out of his fearful state and begins to complete goals again. Or goal completion begins to occur again—it just takes longer than it used to. I find that clients just need to know that I am hanging in there with them and all their fear. I honor their fear as real and stay with them until they are ready to move forward again with their goals. When they do, it seems like they take greater ownership of these objectives. There is power in taking charge of their lives in the face of all their fear.

These fears shouldn't be hidden or avoided as topics of discussion. Perhaps even more significantly, these fears should not be pathologized. Too often in therapy, when a patient expresses a fear, it is seen as a symptom of a deeper issue and is often inaccurately interpreted or used as a tool to dig into the patient's past. In a coaching setting, on the other hand, a banana is sometimes a banana and a fear is sometimes a fear. By that I mean that you have to notice the fear and not pathologize it. In coaching, therefore, the approach is much more practical and respectful and it accepts the fear at face value. It is seen as normal for people to fear change from the familiar.

For this reason, both client and coach must be alert for the signs and symptoms of fear. It takes commitment and accountability to the coach for clients to break through their fears.

As a fireman, Evan was the last person you'd think of as fearful. He was more than six feet tall and muscular, having spent much time in the firehouse gym. He came to coaching because his girlfriend threatened to leave him if he did not learn to talk to her more, treat her more gently, and take her to nice places. She believed he was afraid to show any emotion, and he was not very interesting company.

At first, Evan was very eager to be in coaching. He wanted to learn how to treat his girlfriend better, which he set as his priority goal. However, in coaching he discovered that he lacked relationship skills that most men his age had already mastered. He began to realize that he couldn't treat his girlfriend like his firehouse buddies. Suddenly he became more anxious and told the coach that this process was not for him and he didn't like his girlfriend that much anyway. When the coach pointed out that his statement reflected fears of the unfamiliar, Evan denied any fear. The coach continued to reassure him that any fears were a normal part of the process and that it would soon get easier for him. The coach used weight lifting as an analogy—that coaching also was hard and that it took a lot of persistence and strength-building through repetition.

Evan got it, though he was still fearful. He agreed to continue seeing the coach, and it took about a month, but Evan began to get more comfortable talking about his feelings, thoughts, and goals. He became more adept at courtship skills, and his girl-friend became much more satisfied. He learned to share more about himself and his feelings, automatically making him a more interesting companion. By sticking with coaching through the fear, Evan eventually was able to get past it and eventually reach his primary goal.

In chapter 13 we will further explore Achilles Factors that sometimes resist outcomes in coaching as well.

The following list includes some of the most common atti-tudes and actions clients manifest when they're fearful of the unknown or of change:

- Being late or missing coaching sessions
- Refusal to do much or any of the homework assigned by the coach
- Bad habits and addictions worsening or relapses occurring
- Confidence dropping or feeling more shame regarding slower progress toward goals
- Becoming increasingly judgmental
- Easily angered by the coach
- Wondering if they are going to be fired as the client since they are not doing homework as quickly or as conscien-tiously as before
- Anxiety or depressive symptoms developing or worsening

Here's an exercise that translates these fears into statements that many coaching clients make. Go through the list and check off which ones apply to you. Even if you're not yet in coaching, you can get a sense of if and how your fears might surface during the process. Where you place a check, recognize that this is a likely place around which anxiety will surface during coaching.

☐ When someone starts asking me about areas that are par-ticularly sensitive, I tend to change the conversation.
☐ I've found myself being unaccountably angry when I become anxious.

☐ When I'm asked to change the way I work, I find myself resisting doing things the new way, even though I know I'm putting myself in jeopardy.

☐ I avoid participating in activities I've never done before; I make excuses about why I can't participate that have nothing to do with my fear.

☐ I become nervous when people bring up ideas or points of view that threaten what I thought to be true, and I often judge them harshly.

☐ When I become nervous or anxious because of stressful situations, I seek comfort in my addictions—alcohol, drugs, gambling, and so on.

☐ If I can't master a skill or a task right away, I often feel ashamed of myself and beat myself up in the internal dialogue in my head.

☐ When things go even a little bit wrong in a relationship or at work, I always convince myself that I'm going to be dumped/fired.

Good coaches don't try to fix the fears. It takes time and work to get over them. Instead, they hang in there during times of heightening fears, and this willingness to do so solidifies the relationship with the client. In contrast, because of the power imbalance in therapy, it often results in an unequal relationship, where the patient talks and the therapist listens and sometimes judges and interprets. The relationship is therefore unbalanced. In coaching, there's a feeling of we're both in this together. By helping clients overcome their fears over a period of time, coaches also help them learn how to be resilient and deal more effectively with other types of fears that arise later.

Manage Bad Habits and Addictions

One way to see the difference between coaching and therapy is through the way each approaches bad habits and addictions. In therapy, addictive behaviors are judged and interpreted. They are seen as part of larger patterns and often rooted in some traumatic past event (for example, a patient's alcoholism is traced back to an alcoholic or abusive parent). A lot of time is devoted to exploring the root causes of an addiction.

Coaching is more respectful of the client and more pragmatic in its approach. All I ask of clients with addictions, for instance, is that they manage what is holding them back. There is no judgment, no interpretation. They just need to manage the behavior effectively—whether coming up with a creative solution (such as successfully limiting the number of drinks at each event) or by attending a 12-step abstinence-based program. We discuss how having accountability relationships such as a coach and a 12-step meeting sponsor (for example, a big brother or big sister advisory relationship in anonymous organizations such Alcoholics Anonymous) are keys to recovery. I find that clients who attend 12-step meetings and work diligently with a sponsor do better in the long run as compared to those who attend meetings alone. There is something about the sponsor and coach relationship that brings out the best in the client.

As a coach, I want to help my clients establish their vision for the next phase of their lives. They can't take this foundational step, however, if they have unmanaged addictions or even bad habits. Repeated behaviors that cause dysfunction, whether involving classic addictions such as drugs, sex, gambling, and alcohol, or bad habits—such as obsessive television watching, Internet compulsivity, or frenetic shopping—need to be controlled. Coaching helps people become aware of how these bad habits or addictions get in the way of the vision of their life they're trying to realize. More than that, coaches work with their clients to come up with a plan and action steps to manage these dysfunctional behaviors. As coaches, we're not particularly focused on understanding the cause of addictions as much as on preventing them from being obstacles to a fulfilling, purposeful life. There is increasing evidence that a genetic predisposition can play the key role in the formation of an addict. However, it's also possible for some people that analysis of the causes helps them manage their addictive behaviors, but it varies from individual to individual. Coaches are sufficiently flexible to tailor their approach to fit a client's needs.

Coaches place the highest priority on their client's vision, and that's why I was concerned when one of my clients, Susan, shared with me a new vision of her life, one that no longer included her husband in it. For a number of reasons, she couldn't discuss her desire for a divorce with her husband immediately, and the anxiety that this situation produced was overwhelming. Her anxiety turned into a number of bad habits, including shopping and obsessive housework. During our coaching sessions, it became clear that these behaviors felt out of control to Susan. It was how she coped with a marriage that was difficult for her. More than that, these bad habits were enabling her to postpone her implementation of her vision. As long as she kept shopping and neatening her house obsessively, she was able to delay the confrontation with her husband and maintain the status quo. During our coaching sessions together, I worked with Susan to develop a plan that would help her communicate with her husband openly and manage these bad habits. Doing so was a critical step, and she began to talk to him about her plans and found that her bad habits decreased in intensity.

Today, Susan is single and a much happier, more fulfilled person and making progress in both our coaching sessions and her life toward fulfilling her wishes.

Sometimes a bad habit or an addiction just needs to be managed with an effective plan in coaching. This is true for Internet addiction, gambling, sex, alcoholism, drug use, and other issues such as procrastination, tardiness, sloppiness, hoarding, sarcasm, anger, lying, compulsive shopping, and many others. At times, a recovery program needs to be involved for the client to have a positive outcome. Coaching is very compatible with recovery programs and helps clients manage their lives in general.

In the spectrum below you can see that once an effective plan to manage a bad behavior or addiction was in place, remission was restored.

Spectrum of Managing Bad Behaviors and Addictions

Bad Behavior/Addiction → Plan to Manage It → Remission & Goals Achieved

Now that you have a better sense of what coaching is all about and how it differs from therapy, you're ready to move on to the next chapter of this book, which will assist you in deciding whether to switch from therapy to coaching, mentorship, or a group program. First, though, read the Inspiration and then complete The Truth Exercise. Refer to the client's sample completed exercise. Blog your thoughts in your journal or online.

DR. JOE'S INSPIRATION

"Be accountable and connected to others, for life cannot be lived in a vacuum."

Full Life Exercise

The Truth Exercise

If completely truthful, my coming clean with myself and my coach would reveal one of my truths to be:

_____

_____

One fear I have about revealing the above truth is:

_____

_____

BUCK'S RESPONSE

If completely truthful, my coming clean with myself and my coach would reveal one of my truths to be:

My truth is that I am not really a tough guy, as I try to appear to others.

One fear I have about revealing the above truth is:

My fear is that I will be found out as a weak man by others, for I live in a lot of fear and rarely go for what I really want in life. I want to be a good man, a good husband, and a good father. I want to take risks, but usually I chicken out. I am ready to work hard on this now.

BUCK'S BLOG

As I read chapter 3, I realized that I have sabotaged my progress in life by avoiding accountability—whether it be by avoiding sports in my youth or now avoiding hiring a coach to work toward my goals. I know that once I hire one, I will be held responsible for working hard and progressing toward outcomes. I have spent my life avoiding this. I am tired of this and now commit toward prioritizing my vision and goals within the context of a coaching relationship.

CHAPTER 4

Decide If Your Therapy or Current Approach Is Working

If you don't think you can evaluate your own therapy, think again. Who is a better authority on your progress and performance in life than you? Recognize that with the information provided in these pages, combined with your own instincts and observations, you can make this choice.

I realize that this is a big decision, and that for many who have been in therapy for years, it may seem counterintuitive. After all, traditional therapists tend to keep certain things to themselves, and you may feel that they have a special formula or training that allows them to measure your progress, making you think that you can't possibly know because you're a layman.

As well trained and well versed in their disciplines as many therapists are, they can't read your mind. You possess a huge advantage over any outsider when evaluating the progress—or lack thereof—you've made. If your sense is that you have not achieved key goals, then the odds are you're right. If you still have the same problems that caused you to see that professional in the first place, then it's clear that something is wrong.

It's possible, of course, that you just need a bit more time—another day, another week, another month and you'll have your breakthrough. In most instances, though, people have a sense if they're nearing a breakthrough. They've taken small steps in the direction of solving their problems; they've changed their attitudes; or they've been able to do things they couldn't do before. If you don't have this sense of movement toward solutions, it may be time for a change.

I recognize that many people in therapy believe they're making progress, but it is often progress measured in small insights rather than real life leaps. Let me tell you about Edwin, someone whom therapy helped in one way but not in ways that mattered most to him.

The Story of Edwin: The Loneliness of the Enlightened

Edwin saw a therapist for eight years. In the first year he mostly dealt with his lack of confidence related to finding out he had been adopted. As a result of his work in therapy, he was able to contact his biological mother and formed an excellent new relationship with her. This helped provide Edwin with a more solid foundation on which to construct his life. He gained confidence and was more willing to take small risks in life.

He continued with therapy, though, because he had other issues that persisted. First, he was lonely. While everyone is lonely once in a while, this was a persistent emotional state, one that Edwin had trouble shaking even when he was with other people. Part of the problem was that he was unwilling or unable to let others get too close to him; he reflexively pushed people away when he saw this happening. Though Edwin understood that this reflex was contributing to his loneliness, he continued this behavior. Edwin also was adrift in his career. A midlevel manager for a national retailer, Edwin was perfectly competent at his job, but he found it lacked challenge and that he had settled into a mind-numbing routine. At the same time, he lacked the push to look at other jobs or careers.

Edwin was disappointed that his therapist wasn't interested in addressing these problems directly, but they did spend a great deal of time talking about how, growing up, Edwin sensed that he was different from other children. Though at the time he didn't know he had been adopted, he said that upon reflection there must have been messages communicated from his adoptive parents that he wasn't their biological child. Maybe it was because he didn't look like them or that his mannerisms were so different, but the end result was low self-esteem starting in grammar school and continuing through adolescence.

The therapist helped Edwin grasp how his perceived differences were sources of anxiety and uncertainty in his life, and how they impacted many of his life choices. The therapist was skilled, and Edwin learned a lot about himself during these years of therapy. Each bit of self-knowledge felt valuable, and Edwin was glad to have it. For this reason, he refused to consider stopping the therapy, even though he was still struggling with his career and his loneliness. For Edwin, every insight was a small revelation about himself, and for a long time he had been hungry for such revelations. It seemed beneficial to continue to discover them.

It was only when the pain of loneliness and career problems became greater than the satisfaction derived from the insights that Edwin realized it was time to fire his therapist.

How do you know if it's time to fire your therapist? Let's look at some specific things you can do to make this determination.

Outcome Assessment in Therapy

Think about what your primary goals were when you first decided to go to therapy and what your primary goals are now. More specifically, put those goals in writing. If you just rely on thinking, you may make assumptions that aren't valid.

Translate the following seven investigative inquiries into your answers in your journal regarding outcomes resulting from your therapy:

1. Define your initial goals that prompted you to seek therapy. Identify whether you had clear, concrete objectives— "control my depression," for instance—or if they were more vague—"be happier." If you had more than one goal, list them in order of importance.

2. Define your goals now in the same way.

3. Determine whether your initial goals have been met. If not, consider whether you've made progress toward them. Categorize that progress as "significant," "moderate," or "little or none."

4. Identify the likelihood of achieving your current goals via your therapy. Categorize that likelihood as "good," "fair," or "poor."

5. List how many sessions you've had over what length of time.

6. Note whether your therapist has given you any idea of whether you're making progress; list any milestones or measurable goals that were established and whether you've achieved them.

7. Try to capture what you've gained from therapy in the past and recently in as concrete a manner as possible. Specifically, note if you've learned valuable lessons about yourself and your behavior; if your career, relationships, spiritual life, or other areas have benefited from therapy; and if so, how.

Use your responses to these seven inquiries above to help you evaluate if therapy has helped you make significant progress toward your goals. Be honest with yourself. Don't respond in terms of how you wish therapy had helped you. If you do this exercise objectively, it should provide you with some of the information you need to decide if it's time to switch from therapy to coaching. For example, if therapy helped you progress toward goals at the beginning, but it no longer helps, then it is probably time to move on.

Why Your Therapy May Not Be Working

Annie, thirty-six, has been in therapy off and on for the past eight years. An attractive professional who is dedicated to her job—she just made partner with a large law firm—Annie nonetheless has suffered from a variety of emotional ills that caused her to seek help. She has consistently refused all medication, instead working hard in talk therapy. At times she has been frustrated with the dating scene—she has trouble meeting guys she likes, and when she does, her relationships tend to last no more than six months. Seeing her friends get married and have kids has added to her anxiety. More than that, though, she talks about feeling unfulfilled and unhappy. "I'm just going through the motions," she claims, and wakes up in the middle of the night "feeling terribly alone."

Therapy has been helpful to Annie in that it has allowed her to express her feelings rather than keeping them locked inside. She has learned about the ways she reacts to her feelings that are not helpful to her. For example, she no longer gets angry with others if she is disappointed. However, after all the work in therapy, she still does not feel content with her life, and her unhappiness, anxiety, and loneliness have persisted.

When she came to Full Life, we began working with her to see how she was functioning in all areas of life.

Annie reported a relatively normal upbringing, and there was little evidence of emotional trauma in her past that might be responsible for her current malaise. She also reported a history of working too hard and not having enough fun. Her loneliness was a powerful and destabilizing force in her life, and she no longer received much meaning from her work.

So we focused on Annie's wishes regarding her desired future. From talking with Annie, it was clear that she longed for a connection to a higher power and purpose. She longed for a significant other. She wanted to have more fun.

We first created a plan with Annie that involved her exploring spiritual options such as meditation and attending church services of her choosing. She attended services at multiple congregations in the area, selecting a different one every Sunday, and finally chose a Unitarian church that seemed right for her.

Next, she began to hone her dating skills to be able to date more effectively with more pleasure and resilience. She joined a dating service and placed a profile on a popular dating Web site. She started to have coffee dates with men she met online or from the dating service. She also developed dating and relationship skills as part of the coaching process.

We worked with Annie to find community-volunteering activities that she was interested in, and this involvement enhanced her sense of purpose and spirituality. Annie chose to volunteer at an organization that distributes food to people in need. She made a few good friends while working there as well.

She also identified activities that brought her pleasure and a sense of having fun. She chose to date more, visit more frequently with friends, attend black-tie fund-raisers, visit museums, and see more film, theater, symphony, and opera. She was thrilled to be socializing so frequently.

Within the year, Annie was a changed person. Though she occasionally experienced lonely moments, she found a guy online with whom she is seriously involved; she meditates regularly at a local yoga center; and she is now doing a great deal of pro bono legal work for people from neighborhoods in need, a few miles from where she lives.

People like Annie often make a certain amount of progress in therapy and then get stuck. While it can be tremendously beneficial to express how you feel and trace the origin of feelings, these actions will take most people only so far and no farther. While some therapies are more action-oriented—cognitive behavioral therapy, for instance, helps people escape counterproductive thinking patterns—they generally lack the creative goal orientation and multidimensional behavioral changes of coaching. Therapy may ignore sectors of life that are critical for making progress—spiritual issues, addiction issues, fun, dating skills, career satisfaction, body image concerns, and the like may not be addressed and therefore hold people back from their intended progress.

The Four Questions to See If Your Therapist Is Goal-Oriented

Many people are hesitant to question their therapists or the process itself. They feel they don't have the knowledge or even the right to ask questions . . . or they don't know what questions to ask. To remedy this situation, I've created four questions you can use to supplement your earlier seven-point assessment. As you'll see, these questions are more direct than the assessment, requesting that you discuss your therapy with your therapist.

The following questions are designed to prompt you to confront whether therapy or your therapist is meeting your needs.

The four questions for therapist evaluation:

1. Are you currently heading in the right direction toward outcomes in all areas of life you desire?
2. Does your therapist measure progress toward outcomes?
3. Does your therapist respond when you ask for a new or revised emphasis on goals (for example, adding other approaches or re-prioritizing outcomes)?
4. Does your therapist recognize his or her limitations and at times refer you to other types of services that complement his or her area of expertise?

Before answering the questions using the exercise at the end of this chapter, let me add some issues you may want to consider before formulating your responses.

For question one, determine which of your objectives are being addressed and which are not. Use this as an agenda for discussion in your next therapy session. Have your therapist state his or her perspective, and contrast it with your own. If a major discrepancy exists, that's a significant problem. Maybe you're on separate pages in terms of what you're getting out of the therapy.

In terms of question two, you may find that you've never discussed outcomes in your therapy. Many therapists avoid all talk of outcomes. They will say things such as "talking cures everything," "just be clear regarding your feelings," "process is all that matters," or "goal-setting is ineffective." Take these statements as red flags. Take it as a bad sign, too, if your therapist is limiting discussion of outcomes—if he or she is focusing only on your emotional symptoms and ignoring other areas of your life.

For question three, think about how your therapist responds when you request that he or she pay more attention to a goal that is important to you. Does the therapist respond with an appropriate plan of action that makes you feel heard? If not, do you feel frustrated, angry, blocked? Is it sufficiently frustrating that you are compelled to try something different?

When you ask yourself question four, consider whether your therapist has referred you to other professionals when necessary. Is the therapist willing to admit that he or she lacks expertise in a certain area? Does the therapist suggest that you supplement your work with him or her by seeing a different type of health care professional? Is the therapist willing to acknowledge that you may need assistance in "untraditional" areas, from spirituality to exercise to career?

Take a moment to read the following Inspiration. After answering The Four Questions Quiz at the end of this chapter, evaluate your responses and don't act impulsively. For instance, don't jettison your therapist immediately and leave yourself without any support. Think it through, go slowly, and end the relationship only after honest discussions with your therapist about the issues the quiz raises. If you determine that you want to find a coach instead, wait until you've found this coach before terminating the relationship with your therapist. Or see both of them for a while if you receive their permission. Refer to the client's sample completed exercise. Don't forget to blog in your journal or online.

DR. JOE'S INSPIRATION

"Dare to ask your therapist to help you reach your goals and outcomes. If he or she agrees, stay. If your therapist gets defensive and tells you outcomes are unimportant, bail and find someone who is outcome-oriented."

Full Life Exercise

The Four Questions Quiz: How Your Therapy Is Going

If the answer is no, circle 0. If some degree of yes, circle or underline a number between 1 and 5, with 1 being the lowest rating and 5 the highest.

1. Are you currently heading in the right direction toward outcomes in all areas of life you desire?	0 1 2 3 4 5
2. Does your therapist measure progress toward outcomes?	0 1 2 3 4 5
3. Does your therapist respond when you ask for a new or revised emphasis on goals (such as adding in other or reprioritizing outcomes)?	0 1 2 3 4 5
4. Does your therapist recognize his or her limitations and at times refer you to other types of services that complement his or her area of expertise?	0 1 2 3 4 5

Total Score = _____	Scoring key	
	0	Bail*
	1 to 4	Probably bail*
	5 to 8	Deeply worry
	9 to 13	Worry
	14 to 17	Up to you
	17 to 20	Probably stay

*If you decide to leave your therapist, make sure you have a new coach or other professional in place before ending the relationship. This scale is just an approximate recommendation. This cannot be decided by anyone but you.

BRUNO'S RESPONSE

1. Are you currently heading in the right direction toward outcomes in all areas of life you desire?	0 1 <u>2</u> 3 4 5
2. Does your therapist measure progress toward outcomes?	0 1 2 <u>3</u> 4 5
3. Does your therapist respond when you ask for a new or revised emphasis on goals (such as adding in other or reprioritizing outcomes)?	<u>0</u> 1 2 3 4 5
4. Does your therapist recognize his or her limitations and at times refer you to other types of services that complement his or her area of expertise?	0 1 <u>2</u> 3 4 5
Total Score = **7**	**Deeply worry**

BRUNO'S BLOG

I can't believe I scored only a 7 on The Four Questions quiz. I never fully realized that not working toward my goals is an important issue for me to look at in my therapy. I really want to achieve my goals, so I am going to talk to my therapist about this at our next session. I am going to need to decide whether I will keep working with this therapist. I suppose it will depend on how he responds to me in our discussion.

CHAPTER 5

Give Me One Good Reason to Fire My Therapist

Perhaps you've now discovered at least one good reason to fire your therapist from taking the four questions quiz. It's also possible, however, that the results of your quiz weren't definitive. You may believe that your therapist is doing you some good but isn't living up to your expectations. If you're still on the fence, talk to your therapist about the results of the quiz. If she responds with anger or defensiveness, that's a bad sign. It means she is more concerned with herself rather than with your concerns. If she is dismissive of your concerns—if she says something such as "I wouldn't worry about any of that"—that also suggests she's not focused on what you want to accomplish.

On the other hand, if your therapist responds positively, explains what she hopes the outcomes will be, and agrees to consider other approaches—including coaching—then it's likely she's open-minded and deserves a bit more time. To be honest, though, I suspect you're more likely to encounter the former reaction rather than the latter. If this happens, here is a reminder that I ask you to read now and return to as frequently as you find useful:

It is vital that you have a therapist or a coach who helps you meet your objectives in your life plan. It is challenging work. You need someone who likes to get his hands dirty alongside you as you press ahead toward your goals.

Six Reasons to Fire Your Therapist

Reason No. 1: Your therapist is only 34 percent effective.

Or maybe he's 28 percent effective. Or 37 percent. Whatever the percentage may be, he's delivering way below capacity. If your accountant was operating at 70 percent below his capacity, wouldn't you fire him? With an accountant, of course, this inefficiency would likely show up in errors on your tax returns, audits, and other clear warning signs. In therapy, the signs are more subtle. Again, let me emphasize that many skilled therapists exist, and they are working at peak capacity with certain types of people—especially people who have serious mental disorders. If your issues and goals fall within the normal range, though, the odds are good that your therapist is not providing you with everything you need.

Here's a good litmus test to determine if your therapist is meeting all your needs: do you view yourself as normal or abnormal? If you believe your therapist is doing a complete job, then you probably see yourself as normal and just starting out as a patient. However, if later in your therapy you find you've been shamed and labeled through your diagnosis, you're going to see yourself as one step removed from letting your therapist go. Or do you see yourself as abnormal and find your therapist to be effective, helping you grapple with serious problems consisting of a mental disorder? (Though if that were the case, you probably would not have bought this book unless you are still interested in coaching when you become asymptomatic.)

Here's another way to evaluate if your therapist is operating at peak efficiency: is he resistant to change? Some therapists believe that nothing significant has taken place since Freud died. Change has always been difficult for some people, even if the changes are better. For instance, you probably have friends who still swear by their vinyl records, their '56 Chevys, and their manual typewriters. They are firm adherents of old technologies, stubbornly resisting change. Therapists who cling to traditional methods share this mind-set. They refuse to consider all the developments and improvements since Freud was a young man. Or they have closed their eyes to these developments and don't know the value of coaching and other approaches.

If you're receiving only 33 percent value for your time and money, I urge you to consider alternatives. Part of the reason why some people accept this poor value is that therapy works to a point. When people delve into their past and discover the possible source of a present problem, when they are able to express and understand their deep-seated feelings, they believe they're making progress. And they are! It's a good first step. Fortunately, we now know how to help people take second, third, and fourth steps. Unfortunately, many individuals in therapy don't realize they have options beyond their therapeutic regimen. They trust they will feel progressively better just from the talking. In reality, they will hit a therapeutic wall. When people limit themselves to traditional therapy, they are like the music aficionado who refuses to purchase a digital music player, new speakers, or a state-of-the-art receiver. This person doesn't have to throw out his CDs, turntable, and vinyl records, but he should consider expanding his system. Is your therapist ignoring all the new approaches of recent decades: yoga, meditation, and spiritual pursuits and coaching of all types? If so, you have a great reason to look elsewhere for help.

Reason No. 2: Your therapist isn't God.

People tend to assign their therapists godlike status. As you might suspect, it's difficult to fire God. It may be that your therapist is wise beyond his years, that he is astonishingly insightful and provides you with guidance that feels divine. It's more likely, though, that you've turned him into God because of your own beliefs and background. You may have always believed in therapists as all-knowing beings. It's also possible that your therapist does nothing to discourage this belief. There are therapists who say very little but nod sagely and project an air of great all-knowing insight.

Ask yourself if your therapist has any flaws. For instance, does he really understand what your goals are? Has he ever asked you to articulate them? Has he helped you create a plan to achieve them? Even lowly gods should do this much.

In addition, gods shouldn't be limited, and too often, therapists are severely limited in what they're willing to do. For instance, most will not do outcome-oriented work. I once supervised a therapist who refused to give a client a homework assignment to get physical exercise. This therapist said that asking the client to work out felt intrusive. This same therapist, however, admitted being very comfortable referring a client to a psychiatrist for medications; apparently, intruding on the mind is different from intruding on the body.

It often takes two to tango. In other words, your perceptions of the godlike qualities of your therapist are matched by the therapist's godlike demeanor. In many instances, people come to worship their therapists because those therapists, whether consciously or not, create a mystique that encourages deification. See if your therapist exhibits any or all of the following worship-inducing traits:

- Responds angrily or dismissively when you disagree with something the therapist does or says
- Often listens without comment, nodding and taking notes but refusing to provide you with answers to your questions

- Never says "I don't know" or admits that something is outside his area of competency
- Frequently relies on clinical language (psychological terms) to describe your "problems," labeling your condition with this language and refusing to consider any other possible explanations for your problems
- Rejects the possibility of collaborating with a coach, a religious figure, a spiritual guide, or anyone else to help deal with your issues
- Rarely offers you alternatives for dealing with an issue; expects you to follow one path only
- Generally keeps a poker face during sessions; doesn't respond to your breakthroughs with a smile or other expressions of happiness; doesn't respond to your setbacks with empathy; doesn't offer encouragement and verbal support when you need them
- Speaks to you in a consistently formal, neutral tone, even after years of therapy together in which you have revealed your innermost thoughts and feelings

If these traits feel familiar, you'll appreciate the godlike style of Sean's therapist. Sean was a sheet metal worker who was married for twenty years and had four children with his wife, Dee. Recently he learned that his wife was having an affair with his best friend. Sean confronted his wife and friend and they stopped the affair. However, his wife was unapologetic, leaving Sean feeling heartbroken. He felt like he lost both his wife and his best friend. He became depressed, walking around in a state of grief. It was difficult for him to concentrate at work. He stopped enjoying being around his family. He found he wasn't enjoying sports or anything else anymore. His beliefs about his marriage had been shattered. Finally, he engaged the services of a therapist to help him cope with feelings of hopelessness.

He started seeing his therapist weekly. Immediately the therapist began to accuse him of not being as good a husband as he should have been. In fact, Sean was an excellent husband.

He was a good man, a good father, and a good provider, *and* he loved his wife. However, the therapist began a litany of judgments about how his overall performance was inadequate in his marriage. When he objected to her assumptions and accusations she would shut him down with a comment such as "Who is the therapist here, you or me?" He felt intimidated and gradually felt worse and worse until after several months of sessions, he decided that the therapist was making him worse instead of better.

A friend of Sean's was seeing a relationship coach with his wife, and they were very pleased. Sean engaged the coach's services as well and started to work with her individually. After a few sessions the coach recommended that Sean's wife join them for a few sessions. In these sessions it became clear that Sean's wife no longer loved him and desired to move out. As much as this was not the outcome Sean sought, at least it was clear and the current situation was not blamed on him. He actually found that he soon started to feel better because he realized that the end of his marriage was due to his wife's dissatisfaction and not his behavior. He continued to work in individual coaching sessions, with the goal of becoming single again and eventually starting to date.

Sean realized that the coach had helped him greatly by figuring out what was actually happening and then coming up with a plan of action. He found that his mood and energy improved rapidly once he understood the next steps he needed to take. The therapist he started with was obviously projecting many of her own issues onto him in a godlike manner. Luckily, his core self was strong enough to get out and find an affirming and more humble coach.

Reason No. 3: Your therapist can't assist with what's really wrong in your life.

More often than not, therapists' training and professional practices cause them to commit sins of omission rather than commission. They mean well, but they are unable or unwilling to deal with the issues of greatest concern to you. For instance, a therapist may be helping a client deal with a difficult workplace situation without having much experience with organizational issues and solutions, refusing to make a referral to a colleague with this expertise. Another therapist may believe that spirituality is unimportant and focuses only on the psychological dimension of a patient's problems—downplaying the patient's complaints that she feels empty inside and disconnected to anything larger than herself. It also may be that the therapist has misinterpreted the source of an individual's depression, assuming it is psychological when in fact it is rooted in a negative career event (getting fired), his or her mate's behavior, a specific relationship trauma (breaking up), addiction (alcohol), the death of a loved one (sibling), parenting problems (dealing with a teenager), or all of the above.

Often, a single bad habit or multiple bad habits sabotage a client from reaching his or her goals. This is where traditional therapists fall short. Clients need a plan to actively manage these bad habits. They need to understand what the bad habit is and then be given strategies and tools to limit the unhelpful behavior (anger, addiction, lack of punctuality, procrastination, unsafe sex, eating issues, task and time management issues, and so on).

Collin was a truck driver who was married for thirty years. Recently he developed mild depression and started seeing a therapist, who assumed that Collin's depression was secondary to "hopeless cognitions and ruminations." In fact, Collin was depressed because he was increasingly having sex with women he met on the road and usually did not practice safe sex. He was worried about how out of control he felt—not to mention that he was repeatedly breaking his marital vows and endangering both his wife's health and his own. However, the therapist never asked him about his behaviors and interests while he was on the road. The therapist taught cognitive therapy at a nearby university and had a tendency to explain all symptoms as having a cognitive causation. Therefore, the real etiology of the hopeless feelings and shame went undiscovered by the therapist because he never bothered to get to know his client better.

Reason No. 4: Your therapist can't coach you to greatness.

When it comes to most life challenges, people need a coach a lot more than they need a therapist. They want someone to help them articulate their vision for their lives; they need someone to help them create a plan to achieve that vision; they require an individual to inspire and motivate them as they move forward; and they want a responsible person to monitor their progress and suggest course corrections when they stray from the path they've set.

Mae has been in therapy with the same therapist for ten years. In the early years, the therapy was very effective in helping Mae better understand herself as well as her family of origin. It also helped her feel better and understood. As the years went by, Mae started to yearn for a more outcomes-oriented process. She was interested in finding a mate and building a career she would enjoy and find meaningful. However, whenever she asked the therapist to help her with these goals, the therapist politely refused by saying she didn't work that way, that she saw her role as simply to help Mae clarify feelings and thoughts, not work toward Mae's goals. It took another year, but Mae eventually found a coach and left therapy behind. Today, Mae is happily married and runs a dynamic Web site commerce business from home.

Like Mae, many people go for years without seeing this refusal to discuss goals as a reason to fire their therapists. To evaluate if your therapist is helping you achieve greatness, answer the following questions:

- Has he ever asked me about my vision for my future? Has he encouraged me to talk about how I see my life five or ten or fifteen years from now?
- Has she worked with me to create a plan to achieve this vision? Does she take what I want for myself seriously enough that she has helped me construct a step-by-step approach to achieve this life goal?

- Does my therapist motivate and inspire me? Does he give me pep talks when I'm down or facing an obstacle? Does he tell me stories that help me see how others have overcome similar obstacles?

- Does she periodically ask me to update my progress toward achieving my vision? Does she help me focus on specific things that have been accomplished as well as things that have not been accomplished? Does she make it easier to measure my forward movement toward my goal?

- Is he willing to suggest specific changes I might make if I'm not making progress toward my goal? Does he come up with practical ideas I can put into effect and that help me get back on track?

If you can't answer yes to these questions, then this is a good reason to fire your therapist if you want someone to help you achieve greatness in your life.

As an alternative, of course, you could ask your therapist to shift to a more goal-oriented approach. If your therapist is willing to do so, terrific. If not, then you're missing out on assistance that is most likely to help you live the life you want.

Reason No. 5: Your therapist is focused on process rather than outcomes.

In most cases, a therapist's greatest error of omission is not paying enough attention to a client's vision and goals. By not coming up with a plan to achieve these outcomes with the client, the therapist often disregards outcomes and simply engages in talk and process. This is the biggest difference between therapy and coaching. Therapy traditionally has valued process and devalued outcomes. Coaching values process, but the strong emphasis is on outcome completion. In coaching, process functions for the outcome's sake. Many or even most therapists believe process is to be valued on its own merits. This is a major theoretical difference. Another difference is that coaching tends to follow the lead of the client, and therapy is dictated by the therapist's assessments and judgments. In other words, success in coaching is measured by achieving the goals that an individual has set forth. If you're tired of just talking without achieving anything, it may be time to switch to a coach.

Obviously, if you're deluded or seriously depressed, your wishes may be unrealistic and compromised. If you believe you should be president (unless you are actually running, of course), if you are sure there is a plot against you (without any evidence), or if you are romantically obsessed with an ex-spouse who has made it clear that he or she wants nothing more to do with you, the goals you create may not be achievable. More to the point, they may be goals built on a missing sense of reality. If this sounds like your problem, therapy is probably the best approach.

Reason No. 6: Your therapist's expertise is too narrow.

Your coaching options are more varied than you might realize. The Internet, the spirituality movement, the notion of work as a potential calling, the belief that honing skills can enhance life, the breakthroughs in physical wellness—all have produced coaches with different areas of expertise. While not all of these individuals call themselves coaches, they all do the essential work of coaching. Some help people achieve their potential through meditation and martial arts. Others work virtually, providing all sorts of online helping services. There are coaches who specialize in careers, while others are much more holistic in their approach. Good coaches may have different approaches, but they share the view that their clients are not sick, damaged, or flawed. They grasp that the people they're working with are quirky, fascinating, and strong.

Think about whether you're frustrated by your therapist's narrow range of expertise. Do you sense you might learn and grow if you ventured outside that narrow band? Do you want to explore meditation to relieve stress, or see if membership in a spiritual community meets your deeper needs? If so, this might be the time to learn about your alternatives.

Don't take it as a given that you require ten years of intensive, self-based therapy to make marginal improvements. Recognize your capacity to make leaps in personal growth and achieve vital goals through coaching, meditation, joining community groups, or pursuing other nontraditional healing alternatives. By changing your perspective regarding what your potential is, you free your-self from self-imposed and socially influenced limits on what you can accomplish.

Next Steps: Just because It's an Alternative to Therapy Doesn't Mean It's a Good One

If you've found a good reason to fire your therapist, proceed with caution to the next step. Too often, people view alternatives to therapy as panaceas, and they're invariably disappointed. You can choose the wrong alternative—a spiritual guru when what you really need is a coach. Or you can expect the approach you choose to transform your life, when in reality it can only impact your life to a point. Or the person you choose is unqualified. All sorts of unqualified people are hanging up shingles. You know they're unqualified if they promise quick fixes and easy answers. Positive thinking, for instance, is often sold as a cure, just as snake oil used to be sold—*"If you learn to be positive in the moment you can get all your wishes to come true! If you visualize money, it will come! If you use your willpower, you can prevent yourself from contracting a disease!"* If only it were that easy! What is missing with these approaches is teaching the importance of strategy, focus, humility, and discipline *over time* in attaining goals. The seduction of positive thinking usually leaves the actual imple-mentation of change and follow-through out of the process. If there is no mention of how to implement change, be concerned. You are being had.

Georgiana was feeling dissatisfied with her life in general. All aspects of her life felt mediocre. A girlfriend recommended that she attend an orientation for an organization that claimed to help people feel better. She went to the orientation and found that the staff present pressured her a lot to sign up for an intro-ductory weekend experience. They kept saying things like, "You need to do this," "Your life will get worse if you don't sign up," and "You really need this weekend." Because of the intense pres-sure, Georgiana almost signed up, but she realized that if their method was really that good, they would be talking about solu-tions and not pressuring her to sign up. Instead, Georgiana hired a coach she had met sometime earlier for one-to-one coaching to address her goals.

If you end up with one of these unqualified people or organi-zations, remember that you can fire your spiritual guide or your wellness guru just as easily as you can fire your therapist. The points raised earlier in this chapter suggest a lot of reasons for doing so.

Ideally, forewarned is forearmed. With the knowledge you now possess, I would expect that you'll find a coach or some other expert who can help you achieve your life goals.

Enjoy the following Inspiration and then complete The FYT Pro and Con Exercise. Refer to the client's sample completed exercise. Blog your thoughts in your journal or online.

DR. JOE'S INSPIRATION

"A normal person chooses between utilizing outdated modalities such as therapy or moving into the future of coaching's new ideas."

Full Life Exercise

The FYT Pro and Con Exercise

List the reasons for being for (pro) or against (con) firing your therapist.

Fire your therapist?

Pro:_____

_____

Con:_____

_____

MELANIE'S RESPONSE

Fire your therapist?

Pro: She always gets defensive when I ask her about reaching my goals. She says goals don't help the process. She says just talking takes care of all my needs.

Con: She is very warm and supportive. She has been there for me like no other.

MELANIE'S BLOG

I can't believe I have to decide whether to fire Ellen, my therapist. What do I know, anyway? Well, for one thing I know if I am reaching my goals, and I am not. Ellen is always saying my goals are not important. Talking about what I am feeling is what is important, she says. I don't trust her answers to my questions when it comes to my goals and me.

If I leave her, I will miss her. She has been a great help for several years. She got me through a few years of depression, but now I am ready to work hard on reaching my goals in all areas of life.

CHAPTER 6

Transitioning: When You're Thinking about Making the Switch

It's usually an awful feeling when you realize you are in a relationship with a friend where your needs are not being met, or they were at one point but they aren't anymore. This is the same thing that happens when you are working with the wrong person in therapy or you have simply outgrown him or her. If it is a person you have grown close to or come to depend on, moving on is an even more difficult reality to swallow. As much as you might like to make a change, you find yourself unable to take action. Or you're able to fire your therapist, but you're unable to start a new relationship with a coach or other helper—it feels like a betrayal, and you hold back.

This is a similar situation to other relationships you may have outgrown—whether significant other, friend, mentor, or boss;

many of us find comfort with the familiar or grow dependent on those we care for, so we often have trouble cutting the cord or starting a fresh professional relationship.

Transitioning from therapist to coach takes a bit of reflection. You need to be honest with yourself about your attitudes toward both therapists and coaches. While this makes sense in the abstract, it's sometimes tough to do in the real world. Your biases—conscious as well as unconscious—can make the transition difficult. As a result, you may end up betwixt and between, unable to continue with therapy but unwilling to move on to coaching.

For this reason, I'd like you to examine the following statements that reflect bias and see which ones apply to you:

- Problems can be solved and obstacles overcome only if you spend the time necessary to delve into the underlying feelings.
- As much as I respect coaches, I don't believe they have the training or the skills necessary to help people the way therapists can.
- I can't help but think about sports coaches when I think about seeing a coach; I just assume they provide a lot of rah-rah encouragement and not much else.
- The issues I have are too huge for any coach to deal with effectively.
- Coaching might be fine for people who need help with their careers or want to date more people, but I can't imagine seeing a coach for what's bothering me.
- I really think a coach might help me, but I have a lot of friends who are therapists, and I don't think they'd approve.
- I've already spent a lot of money on therapy, and it didn't help. If I start seeing a coach, I figure I'll just throw good money after bad.
- After ten years of therapy, I feel emotionally exhausted. I don't think I can take starting over with an entirely new process and having to educate a coach about what I've been going through.

If one or more of these statements apply to you, recognize that your assumptions and preconceptions can prevent you from achieving your life goals. I know it's not easy to get past some of these beliefs, especially if they've been ingrained over the years. At the same time, I've seen many clients who have overcome them, often just by learning more about their own attitudes and prejudices. To that end, let me share some stories of people who have been caught in that transition between therapy and coaching.

Learn to Accept a New Kind of Help

Marie was an ideal coaching candidate. She'd been in therapy five years earlier for about six months, and though she didn't think it was worthless, she didn't believe it had much impact on the challenges she was facing. When she had started therapy, Marie worked as a corporate lawyer, earning a healthy six-figure salary, and was in a strong relationship with another lawyer. Marie's problem was that her life seemed disconnected and meaningless. She had tried returning to the Catholic faith of her youth after ending her therapy, but that didn't dissipate these upsetting feelings. She had eventually married the other lawyer and they had a child, and though these experiences were tremendously rewarding, Marie still felt adrift.

A friend told Marie about a coach she knew who was skilled at helping people discover purpose and meaning in their lives. The friend said that the coach was happy to allow her clients to talk to prospective clients, and that the coach had a Web site that people found helpful. Reluctantly, Marie visited the Web site and talked to a few clients. Both experiences impressed her, and she knew that this coach must be good at what she did.

But Marie refused to call this coach and make an appointment. The problem: Marie was an athlete in high school, and she had a series of coaches who browbeat her. They were the classic screaming, intimidating type of coaches, and it made her want to avoid coaches in any setting. Cognitively, Marie recognized that all types of coaches existed, and that the one her friend referred her to seemed nothing like her high school athletic coaches. Yet her bias was so deep that she couldn't get past it, and as of this writing, Marie still hasn't entered coaching.

Some people are stuck in this transition period for other reasons. After firing their therapists, some individuals take a lot of pride in not being in therapy and work on living their life without outside help. This new independence can serve some people well. Others, though, reach a very humbling and unexpected point down the line when they feel they can't do it on their own anymore and need some expert advice. It's only when they reach this difficult emotional state that they can make the transition to a coach. Let's look at two individuals who were in this type of situation—one person who reached this state, and one person who didn't.

Esther grew up in a Mexican American family on the West Side of Chicago. She was the oldest of five brothers and sisters. Her father worked in a meat-packing plant and was a severe alcoholic. He often screamed and hit Esther when she was a young girl, and she grew up fearing men.

Esther entered treatment with a therapist for three years when she was in her early twenties. At the time she complained of anxiety, decreased confidence, and avoidance of dating. The therapy was very helpful to her in learning about family dynamics and understanding the effects and emotional legacy of having a verbally abusive and alcoholic father. Esther became aware of her fears of men and expectations of disappointment in relationships. She learned that underneath her anger at her father was sadness.

Despite this learning, Esther's therapy was not successful in getting her to be less fearful or to begin dating. Turning her new awareness into confidence in dating was not one of the achieved outcomes. After a few discussions with her therapist, Esther said she was stopping therapy and going to work on these issues on her own. One of the first things Esther did was gather her courage and accept a date from a man she met at a bar. Unfortunately, the date was a disaster. Esther found him crude and mean-spirited, and at one point during the date she lost her temper, called him a jerk, and told him, "This date is over!" It would have been use-ful if Esther had a coach whom she could talk to about this experi-ence and create a dating plan that would take advantage of her self-awareness and help her achieve her goals. Esther, though, was stubborn and convinced she could handle dating on her own. She went on two other bad dates—not disasters, but not very pleasant experiences—before she decided dating wasn't for her. As a result, she remained frustrated and unhappy about her inability to meet someone and form a lasting relationship. To this day, Esther is still single and has given up dating.

Unlike Esther, Buzz was always confident and a little cocky. He was a star athlete in high school and an A student as well. He was handsome and popular with his peers. He attended an Ivy League college and always had a girlfriend. He eventually got married to his college girlfriend, went to medical school, and became a surgeon. He had three daughters, and all was picture-perfect until he was forty-two years old and his wife left him for another man and requested an immediate divorce. He granted her request, but he was shattered and soon became depressed.

Buzz started seeing a psychiatrist, who gave him an anti-depressant medication. This helped him overcome his depression, and he saw a therapist as well for almost a year. Like Esther, their conversations gave him insight into why he chose and married the wrong woman for him and why he didn't see the warning signs that the marriage was falling apart. Despite these insights, Buzz refused to start dating after the divorce. Though he wasn't depressed any longer, he wasn't particularly happy. When he thought about dating, he sometimes fantasized about finding "the perfect woman," but he was terrified of being dumped again. Buzz did, however, recognize that his therapist wasn't doing much for him and wasn't interested in creating a strategy to deal with his dating issues. So he fired his therapist.

At first, Buzz refused to seek help from a coach or anyone else. He figured that he was a smart, successful, and good-looking guy, and his pride prevented him from contacting a coach who specialized in dating and relationships. He believed he could handle something as simple as dating on his own.

Only he couldn't. Unlike Esther, he didn't even try to date. Every time he met someone and thought about asking her out, he found himself paralyzed by the thought of all the things that might go wrong.

Fortunately, his best friend had been through a similar situation—a messy divorce—and he had seen a coach to help him figure out a plan for finding a new relationship. After a number of discussions, Buzz's best friend convinced him to try talking with the coach. In the coaching sessions and from the homework he received, Buzz worked on identifying qualities in women he now sought and those he wished to avoid in the future. In about six months, he no longer felt sad and slowly began to date with the help of his coach. He found he truly enjoyed getting to know other women, and his new dating skills helped him to be comfortable and enjoy the dates. After a year, he met a woman to whom he was greatly attracted. Soon they became more serious and eventually married, and they've been happy for two years and counting.

Beat Inertia and Get Active in the Coach Selection Process

Whether you try to function without assistance or are unable to act on your desire to find a coach, you probably suffer from post-therapist inertia. If you've been in therapy for years, you may feel emotionally exhausted. The idea of starting over with a new person who knows nothing about you can be enervating. Switching from therapy to a coaching process might seem to require energy you lack.

What can reenergize you, though, is becoming actively involved in exploring your options for help after parting ways with your therapist. It is vital for normal people to be educated regarding the different choices for coaching, such as life coaching, executive coaching, men's group coaching, women's group coaching, sports coaching, and spiritual advising. The more you learn, the more likely you'll find someone who is right for you . . . and be excited about that discovery.

To become involved in a search for a post-therapy coach, the take-charge tool at the end of this chapter is your means to assess the different coaches under consideration. This questionnaire lists your priority goals for the coaching and asks each coaching candidate how she would help you achieve each of these priorities. You'll be amazed regarding the range of answers to the same questions and how it galvanizes you to make a fresh start by selecting the best candidate. You'll feel empowered as an active participant in the selection process rather than being a passive patient. You will play a more active role in whom to choose as a coach to facilitate your personal work.

At the very least, you will no longer feel like you are a victim of forces larger than yourself; you'll realize that with greater involvement you can impact not just the course of your healing and life planning but also the speed of your progress. And you will realize that by being actively involved in the selection of the coach as well as the type of specialty coach, you can generate the momentum to find someone who can really help you rather than just wishing that this person would magically appear.

The coaching exercise at the end of this chapter is a questionnaire you can use when you interview various coaches. Use a separate questionnaire for each person you interview. The questionnaire will help you measure the responses of different coaches relative to your prioritized goals. By comparing the scores each coach receives, you can identify the person best able to help you achieve your goals. I think you'll find that using the questionnaires will help you decide about which coach to choose. This selection process also gives you a clear voice for who you are looking for as a coach and what your goals are.

Recycling Therapists

Therapy can be like a drug. Even if you vow to stop, you become anxious during the transition. Without a therapist, you feel lost. Even if you're aware that therapy isn't helping you achieve the life goals you have established for yourself, you've been in that transition and don't like it. Therefore, you end up finding yet another therapist who provides you with talk therapy rather than helping you achieve the career, spiritual, physical, or other goals you've prioritized. I've seen people cling to their roles as passive patients, even when they sense they need more than what their therapy is giving them.

Charlie, for example, had been going to the same social worker, Jean, for six years. Charlie had great respect for Jean, and she had helped him overcome some of his anxieties that had caused problems in his career and his relationships. Yet he had made only a few improvements and remained dissatisfied with these areas of his life as well as others. For a long time, Charlie had suspected that he was on the wrong career path—he was an accountant and good at it, but he longed to be in a more people-oriented field. Charlie also was overweight, and though his therapist had encouraged him to exercise, she provided few suggestions in this regard. For three more years, he kept going to Jean because of his dependence, fondness for her, and passive mind-set. He didn't realize that he had to take back the power he had given to Jean and make his own decisions about what was right for him. He needed to begin developing the necessary skills to address his key unmet goals of career dissatisfaction, relationship success, and body wellness if things were going to change for the better.

Despite this knowledge, Charlie was stuck. He had heard about coaches and how they helped their clients, and Charlie suspected that a coach might be exactly what he needed. But the pull of being a passive patient under the care of a familiar therapist was powerful, so he continued with his sessions with Jean despite the lack of progress toward his goals.

Don't be like Charlie. Force yourself to assess whether you're stuck in a passive patient mode. To conduct this assessment, answer the following:

- Do you acknowledge to yourself that you would be better off with a coach but find yourself unable to leave your therapist?

- Have you fired one therapist only to run through a series of other ones but haven't made significant life progress with any of them?

- Do you find yourself feeling like you're making progress during the therapy sessions, but later find yourself realizing that your life is not changing in the ways you want?

- Have you fired your therapist but are anxious about becoming an active participant in designing your life—an active role that coaching requires?

- Have you been unable to make an appointment with a coach because you feel it is a betrayal of all those years you spent in therapy, that it is an admission that much of the time and money you spent weren't worth it?

- Do you acknowledge that coaching would be beneficial but come up with 101 excuses for not contacting a coach—excuses such as, "I'm not the type of person who can be coached" or "My therapist warned me about how coaching is superficial and ineffective"?

Finally, give yourself a pep talk. Tell yourself that just because you've been passive in the past doesn't mean you have to be that way in the future. It's not easy generating the momentum to hurdle the obstacles that keep you from making progress in your life, but I suspect that the following Inspiration and the Take-Charge Questionnaire might help. Make copies of the exercise to use when you interview potential coach candidates about your future work. Refer to the sample completed exercise. Blog your thoughts in your journal or online.

DR. JOE'S INSPIRATION

"When it's your life plan at stake, you have the right to get what you need from a coach."

Full Life Exercise

Take-Charge Questionnaire

Use a blank questionnaire for each potential coach or therapist you interview.

(Write name of coach or therapist here: _____)

Ask a potential coach or therapist: "How can you help me achieve my priority life goals?" (If not at all helpful, circle or underline 0. If some degree of helpful, circle or underline one number between 1 and 5, 1 being the lowest rating and 5 the highest.)

Priority Goals	Coach's or Therapist's Response	
		0 1 2 3 4 5
		0 1 2 3 4 5
		0 1 2 3 4 5
		0 1 2 3 4 5
		0 1 2 3 4 5
		0 1 2 3 4 5
		0 1 2 3 4 5
		0 1 2 3 4 5
		0 1 2 3 4 5
		0 1 2 3 4 5

Total score: _____

PETULA'S RESPONSE: HER THERAPIST

Priority Goals	Therapist's Response						
Meet a boyfriend	I don't deal with that.	<u>0</u>	1	2	3	4	5
Apply for grad school	You will have to do that by yourself.	<u>0</u>	1	2	3	4	5
Deal better with family pressures	We can discuss your feelings about family.	0	<u>1</u>	2	3	4	5
Better nutrition and weight loss	We can explore your feelings about food.	0	<u>1</u>	2	3	4	5
		0	1	2	3	4	5
		0	1	2	3	4	5
		0	1	2	3	4	5
		0	1	2	3	4	5
		0	1	2	3	4	5
		0	1	2	3	4	5
		0	1	2	3	4	5
		0	1	2	3	4	5
		0	1	2	3	4	5

Total score: **2**

PETULA'S RESPONSE: COACH CANDIDATE

Priority Goals	Coach's Response						
Meet a boyfriend	We will work on dating skills and guidelines, including how to meet a great guy.	0	1	2	3	<u>4</u>	5
Apply for grad school	You can do a school plan with me for the steps to apply to grad school.	0	1	2	3	<u>4</u>	5
Deal better with family pressures	We will develop more adaptive ways for you to deal with your family.	0	1	2	3	<u>4</u>	5
Better nutrition and weight loss	We will come up with a food plan as well as a health and weight-loss plan.	0	1	2	3	<u>4</u>	5
		0	1	2	3	4	5
		0	1	2	3	4	5
		0	1	2	3	4	5
		0	1	2	3	4	5

Total score: **16**

PETULA'S BLOG

I am totally freaked that I may leave my therapist. When I asked, "How can you help me achieve my priority life goals?" my therapist scored a 2, while the coach I interviewed scored a 16. Obviously that means I have to work with the coach if I am going to gain the skills and momentum to build the life I deeply want.

CHAPTER 7

Choose the Right Coach for You

Now that you have a good grasp of what the coaching process entails, and you have begun asking coach candidates how they can help you address your priority goals, you are prepared to choose the right coach to orchestrate that process. Throughout the book I've noted how people often find themselves dissatisfied with therapy because they've chosen the wrong therapist. But it's also possible to choose the wrong coach. In fact, because coaches often have very different training, backgrounds, and areas of specialization, you need to be especially vigilant as you search for a coach to hire. While you obviously know that it makes no sense to hire a career coach if you're primarily concerned about relationship issues, you need to stay focused on your priorities.

There also are nuances to take into account that involve your personality style as well as your goals. If you have a strong-willed, aggressive personality, you may need a coach who is calm and accommodating, someone who doesn't feel threatened or defensive in response to who you are. Similarly, if you need help in a variety of spheres, you may require a coach who has a broad background and can counsel you about everything from religion, to volunteering, to couples enrichment, to business growth.

The key is to approach the hiring process with an open mind. You may have a friend who swears by his coach, but you can't assume that what's right for your friend is right for you. Be aware, too, that you may have some lingering prejudices from your therapy experiences. Even if the "talking cure" didn't take, you still may be drawn to a coach who likes to talk. The real task is to choose a coach who is compatible with your personality and who can help you beyond the sphere of Self, into the ten other spheres, or at least the spheres you want to target.

Remember that there may be times when you decide to self-coach for a while. There are times when you don't need an outside coach and can function for yourself in that role. But be aware that there may come a time when you do have to hire the right person to serve as coach and a relationship of accountability for you to achieve your goals.

Before narrowing down your search to a coach who is a good match for your personality and needs, let's examine some of the key traits any good coach should have. As you'll see, these traits are somewhat different from the characteristics therapists tend to possess.

The Qualities of an Effective Coach

Here is a list of qualities a good coach should possess, and if you find someone with each of these qualities, you at least know your coach has many abilities that will serve you well:

Bears witness A sympathetic ear is highly therapeutic. Sometimes healing comes from speaking with someone in confidence about issues that are rarely discussed. For hundreds of years, clergy have served this role; then therapists; and more recently, coaches have taken it on. Being "seen" and understood feels very good to most people. I should add, however, that bearing witness does not mean bearing judgment. Some people complain that their therapists listen well but then diagnose them and categorize them, and that this strikes them as a form of judgment. You want someone who can listen empathetically but without making you feel as if there's something seriously wrong with you. When you meet with prospective coaches for the first time, evaluate whether they get what you're telling them. Do they simply tell you how they'll help you, or do they restate the issues you've raised so you know they heard you? Do they demonstrate that they've not only heard the words you've said but also the underlying concerns those words expressed or implied? In their presence, do you feel judged or validated?

Communicates effectively   Some therapists are not active talkers and fail to communicate effectively through their facial expressions, body language, and words. At times they just sit there and don't respond. This unresponsive demeanor comes from the long-standing tradition of being *neutral* with a client, not active; process-oriented, not outcome-oriented. With coaches, look for someone who offers the right mix of listening and talking—where you feel heard and receive just the right amount of feedback as well. Pay attention to how a coach deals with your questions during your preliminary interview. If he just talks—or if he just listens—then he probably isn't a particularly effective coach. Try to find someone with whom you feel you've established a helpful dialogue. It's the same thing that happens with a good friend—you establish a rhythm in your conversations where you feel you're being heard and that you're hearing your friend.

Fosters accountability   People perform better in relationships where they are held to specific standards. Just as an athletic coach expects his players to meet certain requirements in schedules, training regimens, and game performance, your coach should expect similar things from you. Ask prospective coaches if they will hold you accountable for achieving goals set during coaching sessions, and ask them how they will hold you accountable—will there be regular reality checks to determine if you're making progress? Remember, if you've been in therapy for a while, you were not held accountable. In fact, you may have assumed that you'd need to be in therapy for years before you saw results. Your therapist may never have asked you if you've been moving toward achieving an objective at work or in a relationship. Your coach should call you on behaviors that demonstrate you're not making progress. You want your coach to challenge you, to demand that you move forward.

Harper was in coaching for two years. At first, she was very ambitious and achieved key goals during the first year. Then she started to resume some of her bad habits and stopped working toward her goals. For example, she had lost fifty pounds, and during the second year she put all the weight back on and more. At first her coach allowed a bit of a backslide, since behavior change is difficult. But when she started to backslide in other spheres besides Body, he brought up his concern to her in a session. It was as if she had stopped prioritizing her desired outcomes. Harper cried when they discussed her not working toward *her* goals. At the end of the session she recommitted to her overall plan and took responsibility for her backward steps. The coach didn't hold Harper accountable in a mean or insensitive way. Instead, he gently but firmly reminded her what her goals and commitments were and his concern that she wasn't keeping those commitments. By being both empathetic and insistent on accountability, he motivated Harper to acknowledge her backsliding and to do something about it.

Presents minimal distractions   What does a coach's office look like? When you meet with him for the first time, are there any interruptions? Does he go off on tangents that are unrelated to the topic at hand? You need to be able to concentrate during your coaching time, but if you're in an environment where distractions are common, this won't happen. For example, the office should be clean, quiet, and comfortable. You should feel you have 100 percent of a coach's attention. He or she should not take phone calls during your session. Your coach should have stringent professional boundaries, like no inappropriate touching or socializing outside of your coaching sessions. Almost all of the conversation should be about you and not the coach. If the coach does refer to himself, it should usually refer to a topic that is being discussed related to your coaching goals. After you interview the coach, ask yourself how easy it was to concentrate on your issues. Did your attention wander? If it did, was the coach able to bring you back to the key topics?

Preston was a thirtysomething young man who was seeing a coach for six months. He was working on leaving his current sales position and landing a new, more meaningful sales job. The coach was an attractive, middle-aged married woman. Preston liked her energy and made progress in the coaching toward his goals. However, during their sixth or seventh session, the coach began reaching over and holding his hand for a moment when he would become angry or regretful about what he was talking about. It seemed an innocent gesture, and to be honest, Preston appreciated the empathy. Yet, he became a little uncomfortable as the touching escalated—his coach would hug him at the start and the end of their sessions. He noticed, too, that his coach had taken to staring deep into his eyes, not like a clinician trying to probe his thoughts but like she was coming on to him. Nonetheless, Preston continued with the coaching, figuring it was just his imagination. Plus, he had heard that patients sometimes become attracted to their therapists, so he figured he might be sending her the wrong signals. One day, she mentioned that they should try to hold a session at a nice local bar—she said she thought that if they talked in a more open environment, he might be more open when talking about his career dissatisfaction. Preston didn't want to meet at a bar, but he wanted to please the coach, so he agreed to her idea. At the bar, when she reached over to kiss him, he told her that the coaching

was not working well for him and he was going to find someone else.

Exudes humility   Arrogance does not a good coach make. In
plain English, coaches who appear superior, self-centered,
invulnerable, or opaque are not for you. Fortunately, a few min-
utes with these arrogant types gives the game away. You know
right away if the session is more about the coach than you.
As we've discussed, many therapists adopt a godlike, judging
demeanor. In coaching, you want someone who facilitates your
agenda; gives up judgment; admits mistakes; accepts questions;
and changes his or her approach when change makes sense. A
good litmus test to see if a coach exudes humility is to ask a few
questions. Does the coach brush your questions aside, or take
them seriously? Does he or she make fun of your concerns, or
respond empathetically? Does the coach treat your questions
like they're stupid or like they're intelligent?

     Tate engaged the services of a business coach because he
was developing a new restaurant concept. In the past, he had
sabotaged one of his business ventures because of his fear of
spending money, and he didn't want history to repeat itself.
He also thought he could use someone to bounce ideas off of.
The coach was a well-known, successful, retired executive.
However, when the first session began, the coach never
seemed to stop talking about himself and his own accomplishments. He seemed unable to pay attention to Tate or his aspirations. When Tate asked the coach when they were going to
discuss his situation and his goals, the coach started talking
about himself again. At the end of the session, Tate wisely told
the coach that he would be looking elsewhere.

Displays competence   To a certain extent, you can determine
a coach's competence via your own observations and from
references from people you trust. Ask about their training
and years of experience. Inquire about their areas of interest in coaching. What do other clients of the coach have to
say about him or her? Are people lukewarm in their comments or do they use words such as "helpful," "perceptive,"

"effective," and the like? It's fair to ask a prospective coach for references; he may have a few colleagues and even former clients speak with you or even e-mail you. There are privacy issues regarding provision of references, but coaches, unlike therapists, often provide them because they don't view coaching as some dirty little secret. In addition, use your intuition. At times you can get a sense of someone's competence by talking to him or her. Beware of coaches who brag or make grandiose promises. Be receptive to those who are articulate and passionate about their coaching methods. But each time you talk to a prospective coach, you should be intrigued by something he or she tells you. This is a sign that the coach will be a helpful guide and teacher.

Demonstrates flexibility and resourcefulness   The person you hire to help orchestrate a life-optimization plan must approach it with flexibility and inventiveness. That might mean finding you resources in a specific sphere outside of his or her area of expertise—hooking you up with a community group, for instance, or recommending an expert in mind-body healing, if that's your targeted area. Your coach also needs to be able to adapt your plan if your goals change during the coaching process, or if you've been having trouble achieving overly ambitious goals. Ask a prospective coach if she is able and willing to refer her clients to experts outside of her area of specialization. Does she do so regularly? Why and when does she make these referrals? What does she do when a client is struggling with a plan? How does she handle it? Beware of coaches who say they possess all the expertise any client ever needs and that they never have to revise a plan or make referrals. You want someone who is sufficiently humble in that he recognizes he doesn't know everything. Yet, you also want someone who knows a lot on his or her own.

A Coach Is Like a Private Investigator

At times, effective coaching is like a good private eye investigation: together the coach and client unearth clues, attempt to makes sense of what they mean, and look for a solution to what was formerly a mystery. The coach you hire has to have investigative ability. This means being able to look at information in all spheres and help you come up with a plan that "solves" whatever issues you face and works toward your goals. Some people just have a knack for figuring things out, and you want your coach to possess that knack.

People often come to coaching thinking they know exactly what they want to address. However, sometimes discoveries emerge during the sessions that reveal additional issues that were hidden but that turn out to be very important. For example, a person may come thinking they are single because they haven't met the right person. However, coaching may reveal that the client unknowingly pushes away dates with good qualities. Another example might be that a person continually takes jobs they don't like and pursues careers they find meaningless. They may say they always hate the job they select. However, in coaching, they may discover that they are actually avoiding the truth of what they want to do for their career.

Effective coaching also opens the eyes of the client in unexpected and exciting ways. What you want is a coach capable of fostering eye-opening moments.

When you meet with prospective coaches, consider how perceptive they are about what you say. As you're describing what you're looking for in a coach, do they:

- seem to be able to answer your questions and finish your thoughts?
- suggest ideas for dealing with your issues that strike you as creative or at least different from what you've tried in the past?
- describe similar situations of other clients that demonstrate their ability to figure out tough problems?

Realistically, it's not always easy to identify a coach's investigative ability in one meeting. As you move forward with the coach you choose, though, monitor how well (or how poorly) he or she digs into your issues and comes up with a plan or specific actions that seem more effective than anything you could have created on your own.

Barry was interviewing coaches because he felt stuck in his life and his job. Married for twelve years with two daughters, he was working as an executive for a restaurant management company. Having an affair with a coworker and then going through serious marital problems, Barry believed his career and marriage were going nowhere. Therefore, Barry was confused and concerned about at least two life spheres. He wanted a coach who could help him sort all this out, make good choices, and work toward solutions. Barry interviewed three coaches, and all of them made good first impressions. One was particularly charming and articulate, and at first, Barry leaned in his direction. Ultimately, however, he picked the coach who asked him the best questions and responded probingly to his answers. In his gut, Barry felt that this coach was a guy who was going to be relentless in helping him seek his truth. The coach he selected was probably the least personable of the three, but he was laserlike in his focus on the things Barry wanted to address.

The Four Steps in Choosing a Coach

The previous suggestions all can be implemented on an ad hoc basis. In other words, you can ask questions and make observations when you're interviewing prospective coaches, when you talk to them on the phone or communicate via e-mail, or even during early stages of the coaching process. They offer a way to think about whether a given individual has the skills that a coach requires. Ideally, you'll get most of your questions answered before hiring a coach, since you don't want to waste time and emotional energy by starting to see the wrong coach.

Many coaches require you to agree to a fixed number of sessions, covering three months, six months, or a year, for example. Often you will see a coach for two or three sessions per month. Therefore, recognize the possibility that you could be locked into a certain number of sessions with the wrong coach if you don't obtain all the information you need upfront in order to make a good decision.

Now let's look at a more formal, four-step process that will help you evaluate possible candidates and make a good choice:

Step No. 1: Get referrals from sources you respect

Get as many referrals from people you respect who know at least one excellent coach. These referrals can include friends, physicians, colleagues, other coaches, mental health professionals, coaching organizations (for example, the International Coach Federation), professional associations, and religious family services. In a journal or a notebook, devote at least a full page for your notes and impressions of each coach candidate. Ask your referral sources to tell you why they referred the coach to you. Write down their responses. When all your referrals are in, narrow your referrals down to two or three.

Step No. 2: Call each of the finalist coach referrals

See how they respond to your inquiry. Address the following issues:

- Do they call you back within twenty-four hours? You want someone who calls you back within twenty-four hours on business days. This demonstrates their responsiveness to clients. If they don't do it well with prospective clients, you don't want to be their regular client.
- How do you like the voice mail, the staff, or even the coach on the phone? This tells you a lot about their customer service practices and what it would be like to be their ongoing client. How would you like to be listening and talking to them for full sessions?
- Do they answer your questions well? Again, how do you feel about their responses to any questions you pose?

- Do they have any materials or a Web site for you to review? Web sites are great tools to evaluate a coach. Typically, a Web site not only contains facts about a coach (such as experience, expertise, and credentials) but also gives you a sense of his or her philosophy and attitude—the tone of the writing tells you a lot about a coach's approach to clients.

- Is their initial consultation free, or do you have to pay for it? As long as they tell you there is a charge, that is fine. You probably don't want to work with someone who doesn't charge something for their services.

- Do they lock you into a package of sessions from the very beginning, or is the initial meeting a stand-alone, even if there is a charge for it? The first session should be a stand-alone session. It is fine if the coach asks you afterward to decide whether to commit to a package of sessions (such as two or three per month for three months, six months, or a year).

- What is the no-show and last-minute-cancellation policy? A twenty-four- or forty-eight-hour cancellation policy is standard. Just see if they tell you clearly what the penalties are regarding financial charges. These charges should not be vague.

- Does the coach do face-to-face, telephone, video, or mixed modalities of coaching? In my experience, face-to-face is superior to telephone coaching. Video falls somewhere in the middle. I recognize that many coaches only do telephone work and that it often works extremely well. Executive coaches also prefer telephone or video sessions in certain instances. In my experience, the only clients who seem to like telephone coaching as a first choice are those who never had a face-to-face experience. While there's nothing wrong with coaching via phone or video, these less personal approaches are generally more effective when they supplement face-to-face interactions. For example, you may travel for business frequently. You might see your coach for a long in-person session initially, and then use video or telephone for most sessions when you travel. This is fine. I also recommend a periodic face-to-face session whenever possible. Some clients do this at three-month or six-month intervals. This helps keep a strong connection to your coach.

- How do you feel when connecting to the coach's voice mail, staff, and the coach herself? Again, listen to your intuition regarding your experience. Record your impressions in your journal on the respective page for that coach candidate.

Step No. 3: Narrow the candidates down to two or three

- When examining all the coach candidates, what are their special coaching areas of expertise (such as dating, career, team, organizational, relationship, and life)?
- What training have they received? Was the training long-term or brief? Was the coach's training in person or on the Internet? Did they receive any certification? Do they have clinical training, certification, and licenses in any other fields? Do they have any other qualifications?
- Are there at least three references you can check for each?
- Using The Choose-a-Coach Method at the end of this chapter, narrow the candidates down to the two or three coaches you will see for a single session.

Step No. 4: Choose a qualified coach

- See each of the finalist coach candidates for a single session.
- Again, use the Choose-a-Coach Method at the end of this chapter and the Take-Charge Questionnaire (from the end of chapter 6) to score each coach candidate. Select the coach you want to hire by seeing who scores the highest at each of your one-on-one meetings with the finalists.
- Call the coach you select and make your first appointment!

Personalizing Your Search

I would be remiss if I didn't provide you with some more suggestions about how to find a coach who is right for your particular
concerns. If you're like most people who decide to hire a coach,
you've emerged from a relationship with a therapist having a bit
of skepticism about whether anyone—including a coach—can
really provide you with helpful, practical advice that you
can implement effectively. Maybe you've been seeing a therapist
for years about your overbearing tendencies and how you alien-
ate family, friends, lovers, and work colleagues. Maybe your issues
are broader—you've been working on coming to terms with a
traumatic childhood, you're alienated from the church you grew
up in, and you're overweight. Maybe you frequently talked to
your therapist about vague feelings of malaise or a sense that you
weren't doing what you were supposed to be doing with your life.

Now that you're in the market for a coach, use the burn-
ing issues from therapy to focus your search. You may not have
received much satisfaction from your therapist in addressing these
issues, but they serve as a guide for what's important to you. It may
be difficult for you to formulate specific goals at the moment—as
I noted, the coaching process often reveals goals hidden to clients
initially—but you can use your therapy sessions to think about the
areas or spheres where you'd like to do more work.

This will tell you if you should look for a coach with a strong
spiritual background. Or if you need a fitness coach because body
image has always been a concern. Or if you want a coach experienced in working with people on issues of meaning and purpose.
In this way you can be prepared to see if a given coach has a
background in the area or areas of significant concern to you.

In addition to using the Choose-a-Coach Method at the end
of this chapter and the Take-Charge Questionnaire from chapter
6, you also might try formulating a one-sentence description of
what you want to achieve through coaching. This is a kind
of trial balloon to float with a prospective coach. It may not be a
completely accurate statement of your goals—formulating these
goals can take some time and work—but it will give a coach

an opportunity to think about whether he's right for you. Most coaches will be honest. They'll tell you upfront if they feel they have the capabilities to coach you effectively. For instance, your statement might be, "I have spent years feeling lonely, even during my former marriage, and I want to figure out how to connect with other people." One coach may do a great deal of relationship work and feel comfortable working with you. Another may be more geared toward other spheres and refer you to someone else. At the very least, though, expressing this statement gives the coach a chance to tell you upfront if he's right for you.

Let me conclude this chapter by sharing the story of one person's search for a coach. Donna was a forty-one-year-old, twice-divorced, stay-at-home mother of two kids and had been in therapy for eight years. Donna had grown up as the daughter of a well-known and highly paternalistic judge, and the experience had made her relationships with men difficult, or at least that was Donna's theory as to the cause. While she had made some progress in understanding how her paternalistic father had made it difficult for her to enjoy good relationships with other men, she had not had a good relationship with a man since her second divorce, four years ago. In addition, Donna was a binge eater—her therapist told her that clinically speaking, women don't have eating disorders at her age—and she also became depressed on occasion, feeling like she wasn't giving anything back to her community or to the world at large. Though money wasn't an issue—her second ex-husband was wealthy and had been generous in the divorce settlement—Donna also was interested in finding a career now that her kids were both adolescents.

After Donna fired her therapist, she began searching for a coach, and at first was frustrated by the process. She interviewed her best friend's career coach but found this coach to be too specialized for what she wanted. Donna also talked to a life coach her first husband had used and said was good, but she discovered that the vast majority of his clients were male and that he really didn't understand women.

Donna was frustrated and ready to give up the search when she decided to go online and Google coaches in her area. She came up with a surprisingly large number, but she didn't know how to winnow them down. Fortunately, Donna's ex-college roommate was a social worker who had done some coaching, and she was able to vouch for three of the coaches on the list.

Donna interviewed all three, first calling them and then setting up appointments. The first two were fine, but the third one she visited, a coach and psychologist named Anne-Marie, was perfect. The moment she walked in the office and they started talking, Donna connected easily to Anne-Marie. She was warm, down-to-earth, and open. As they talked, it turned out that Anne-Marie had worked in an eating disorders clinic and that she also was heavily involved in a community group whose work interested Donna. Combined with her psychological training and experience, Donna decided Anne-Marie was the right coach for her, and she has been extremely pleased by her choice.

I related this story to emphasize that even though all the tools I've provided are useful in making a selection, you should also rely on your instincts when you talk with and meet a coach. You should evaluate their experience and expertise critically, but don't ignore your own emotional responses to the individual. Unlike a therapist, a coach will act naturally; he won't don a therapeutic pose. Therefore, pay attention to how you respond. Do you like this person? Does he seem to get you? Are you able to talk easily with him? These are essential questions to consider before you hire a coach.

Enjoy the following Inspiration, exercise, and blog page. I hope that the following Choose-a-Coach Method exercise will assist you in making the right choices. Make copies of the exercise to use when you interview potential coach candidates about your future work. Refer to the sample completed exercise. Blog your additional thoughts in your journal or online.

DR. JOE'S INSPIRATION

"No one can pick a better coach than you can."

Full Life Exercise

The Choose-a-Coach Method

Use this method in selecting the coach you will hire.

Name of coach candidate interviewed: _____

Rate the coach's response to each question, 0 being the lowest rating and 5 being the highest.

Rate how fast the coach or office gets back to you after you called.	0 1 2 3 4 5
Rate the coach's communication style with you—inclusive of voice mail messages, office staff, and/or the coach's style on the telephone.	0 1 2 3 4 5
Rate the overall quality of answers to your questions (refer to the Take-Charge Questionnaire from chapter 6).	0 1 2 3 4 5
Rate the materials available and/or Web site.	0 1 2 3 4 5
Rate how you like the format of the initial consultation (such as full session and fee or no fee).	0 1 2 3 4 5
Rate if you are offered an initial stand-alone session or feel locked into premature choices.	0 1 2 3 4 5
Rate if you are given a clear no-show and last-minute-cancellation policy.	0 1 2 3 4 5
Rate if the coach provides the modality of coaching you prefer (such as face-to-face or telephone).	0 1 2 3 4 5
Rate how you like the coach when talking with him or her on the telephone.	0 1 2 3 4 5
Rate if the coach has expertise in the area of coaching you prefer (such as career, relationship, executive, sports).	0 1 2 3 4 5
Rate their training and credentials.	0 1 2 3 4 5

Rate if they provided you with at least three references.	0 1 2 3 4 5
Rate your overall impression of the coach in the one-to-one session.	0 1 2 3 4 5
Calculate the total score. *Highest score is the coach you want to hire!*	Total score: _____

ADRIANE'S RESPONSE

Name of coach candidate interviewed: Candidate A

Rate how fast the coach or office gets back to you after you called.	0 1 <u>2</u> 3 4 5
Rate the coach's communication style with you—inclusive of voice mail messages, office staff, and/or the coach's style on the telephone.	0 1 2 <u>3</u> 4 5
Rate the overall quality of answers to your questions (refer to the Take-Charge Questionnaire from chapter 6).	<u>0</u> 1 2 3 4 5
Rate the materials available and/or Web site.	0 1 <u>2</u> 3 4 5
Rate how you like the format of the initial consultation (such as full session and fee or no fee).	0 1 <u>2</u> 3 4 5
Rate if you are offered an initial stand-alone session or feel locked into premature choices.	0 1 2 <u>3</u> 4 5
Rate if you are given a clear no-show and last-minute-cancellation policy.	<u>0</u> 1 2 3 4 5
Rate if the coach provides the modality of coaching you prefer (such as face-to-face or telephone).	0 1 <u>2</u> 3 4 5
Rate how you like the coach when talking with him or her on the telephone.	0 1 2 <u>3</u> 4 5

(continued)

Rate if the coach has expertise in the area of coaching you prefer (such as career, relationship, executive, sports).	<u>0</u> 1 2 3 4 5
Rate their training and credentials.	0 1 <u>2</u> 3 4 5
Rate if they provided you with at least three references.	<u>0</u> 1 2 3 4 5
Rate your overall impression of the coach in the one-to-one session.	0 1 <u>2</u> 3 4 5
Calculate the total score. *Highest score is the coach you want to hire!*	Total score: **21**

ADRIANE'S BLOG

I am so excited that I am getting close to selecting the coach I hope to work with. Using the Choose-a-Coach Method, I narrowed the candidates down to three finalists and then saw that Marcy, the coach I am selecting, scored the highest by far. I am so pleased that I was active in this process instead of just working with anyone.

PART II

BUILD THE LIFE YOU WANT ON YOUR OWN AND WITH YOUR COACH

CHAPTER 8

Applying the Spheres:
The Key to Creating
a Full Life

I always tell my clients that they probably can't achieve the life they want alone and that I, as their coach, definitely can't do it alone. No coach can, even if he or she possesses tremendous expertise and experience. As much as I believe in the power of coaching, I can't help someone who isn't willing to help himself.

That's why I've included this section on the spheres. As this chapter's title suggests, these spheres really are the secret for achieving a rich, fulfilling life. Too often, people do a lot of work to improve in one aspect of their lives. They go on a diet and lose a lot of weight and look fabulous, for example. Or they focus exclusively on their career and snag a terrific job. Unfortunately, they neglect the other areas of their lives, and as a result, they still feel lonely, sad, unfulfilled, and lost. The secret, therefore, is to address all or most of the spheres rather than just one or two.

As you'll recall, the eleven spheres represent the full range of life areas, from family to spirit. Originally, I developed Spheres of Life Coaching to serve as an organizing guide for clients to conceptualize their current and future life. The objective was to organize the thinking of clients into doable next steps, starting with an orderly inquiry into eleven areas of life. With my coaching organized around the eleven spheres, I could communicate clearly how to identify strengths, weaknesses, goals, and other useful steps. The first step of the process for a client involves figuring out what's going well and not so well in each sphere.

While it certainly helps to have a coach guide you in this assessment, you can begin some of this work on your own. In fact, the more you learn by yourself, the easier it will be for your coach to help you achieve your goals.

Let's start with a quick definition of the three Big-spheres and the specific smaller spheres that fall into each group:

The You Big-sphere

Self: Importance of individual development, management of life, and confidence. Emotional symptoms also belong in this sphere.

Body: How body image, nutrition, fitness, and medical health relate to wellness.

Spirit: Themes of religion, universal meaning, personal faith, addiction recovery, and connection with something greater than self.

Fun: Pleasurable hobbies and playful activities as vital sources of life energy.

Home: The notion of the place where we live and how it impacts our lives.

The Career Big-sphere

Work: Issues involving jobs and careers, and how work can evolve into a calling.

Money: Financial skills and how they relate to larger issues of emotional well-being.

The People Big-sphere

Love: Everything from dating skills to intimate relationships.

Family: Relationships with children, parents, siblings, and nontraditional definitions of family.

Friends: Forming and fostering platonic relationships that add joy and meaning to life.

Community: Group membership and volunteering for the good of others and how they bring purpose and fulfillment.

As you looked at each of these spheres, you may have instinctively noted where you were having problems as well as where you were fine. That's terrific. Your instincts are often reliable, and you should heed them. At the same time, people are complex. Sometimes you can fool yourself about your strengths and weaknesses in each sphere. Or you may just need help in knowing what to do to strengthen a weak area of your life or even further fortify an existing strength.

For these and other reasons, I'm going to provide you with some insights about each sphere as well as some tools to do productive work in each of them. Before we do this, though, I need to give you a sense of why the spheres are crucial for achieving balance, how they evolved from specific societal developments, and how they helped a guy named Tom achieve a much fuller, more meaningful life.

Finding the Right Balance

It is as if you started an exercise program that only consisted of right-hand arm curls with a twenty-five-pound dumbbell. After a while you would develop a stronger right bicep, but the rest of your body wouldn't be in good shape, and your body would be out of balance. As absurd as this limited exercise regimen may sound, therapists have been working with people in an analogous out-of-balance approach. A multidimensional approach is necessary, and at its best, coaching offers you ways to work on any or all dimensions of your life.

Be aware, however, that it's not just therapy that focuses on one dimension. Some people fire their therapists, but they embark on equally unbalanced approaches to self-healing. For instance:

- When you try to inject more meaning and connection into life by meditating five hours daily, you are limiting your growth to one dimension.
- When you become a workout fanatic because you are depressed about relationships and body image, you expect too much from one healthy activity.
- And when you believe that all your problems will be solved if you find the right relationship or the right career, you are viewing happiness from a narrow and illusory perspective.

Therefore, be careful about what you do after firing your therapist. Be wary of any guru or "ism" that promises a holistic approach yet maintains an extremely narrow focus. When you do work on your own, keep the eleven spheres in mind. I realize how easy it is to become caught up in one area where your biggest hurt is. You become so focused on dealing with your relationship issues or your family problems that you start to think that if you could only fix this one area, everything would be great.

For this reason, concentrate on the concept of balance. Concentrate on it even if you're devoting all your time and energy to one sphere because of a crisis or because you feel unable to do anything else until you deal with a specific issue. As important as a given sphere is, other spheres must be addressed simultaneously or at least eventually.

New Methods for Life Optimization

It's much easier now to work in all eleven spheres than it was ten or twenty years ago. Today, books, articles, television and radio programs, and other media communicate the benefits of every-thing from acupuncture to massage therapy to spas to coaching as ways to overcome problems and gain fulfillment. Our society has embraced alternative health care and incorporated various techniques and tools into the mainstream. People use hypnotism to deal with fears or journey to sacred sites such as Sedona to renew their spiritual energy.

In short, our consciousness has been raised, and as a result, people are ready to redefine working on one's life in a more holis-tic way. Here are some signs of this raised consciousness.

The Growing Awareness and Use of Coaches

Career and executive coaches are ubiquitous in most fields, and personal coaches have adopted and adapted performance-enhancing methodologies to help their clients. They are more goal- and action-oriented than traditional therapists, and their results-oriented focus appeals to many people who have been in talk therapy for years but haven't made much progress in solving their problems or building the life they want. They are now look-ing for someone to help them create and carry out a life plan.

The Spirituality Movement

More people are participating in yoga, learning kabbalah, prac-ticing meditation, studying Buddhism, going on pilgrimages, and seeking connection to universal values and meaning or a higher power. They are recognizing that what is missing in their life may not relate to relationships or careers but to the spiritual side of themselves. Many of you are interested in means of further enlightenment in this age of global warming and violent conflicts between countries. Finding spiritual meaning and connection is very calming and reassuring during these times.

Purpose and Volunteerism

From Habitat for Humanity to AmeriCorps, volunteer options have multiplied. Oprah, former president Bill Clinton, Bill and Melinda Gates, and many other prominent citizens have led the country toward a more giving and "green" mind-set, and many ordinary, caring individuals have joined "do-gooder" and community groups. People are learning that by helping others, you also help yourself; that using your time and talents to help people in need—the homeless, students, the elderly, and the disadvantaged—gives our lives a sense of meaning and purpose.

Work-Life Balance

The increasing recognition that the personal and the professional must be in balance has raised consciousness about living a whole life. People are seeing that work success is not enough. Some women are seeing that it is okay to want achievements beyond motherhood. As a result of all this, hard-working professionals are devoting more time to their families, moms are going back to work, and people are spending more time on hobbies and other interests from which they derive great satisfaction.

The Mind-Body Connection

Massage therapy, exercise, walks in the woods, and other physical activities are no longer seen just as ways to get our bodies in shape, but also as ways to pursue wellness and to feel better about ourselves. Challenging activities such as climbing a mountain or canoe trips in the wilderness heighten our appreciation of the world and inspire us to set other life goals and achieve them with renewed energy.

All these assorted activities and new movements have opened the door to many possibilities for leading a more fulfilling life, one that you might not have been aware of in years past. You are less likely to view life through a one-dimensional lens. You now know that there is more to life than work or parenthood or religion. These are important areas, but there are many more to address as well if you want to optimize your existence.

When you experience a general sense of dissatisfaction or unhappiness or encounter a more specific problem, you now have alternatives beyond traditional therapy. You may not capitalize on these alternatives, though, because you're not sure what is available. There is no plan or precedent to follow; you don't know if you should start meditating or join a community group or hire a coach or go on a wilderness trek. You are not sure how to approach a new and exciting goal and turn it into a reality.

An Example of How a Spherical Approach Works

Despite all the consciousness-raising about life's many dimensions, people often become myopic about their lives, especially when they are under stress or feeling unhappy. They become preoccupied with finding relief and usually fixate on one potential approach. For instance, Tom was suffering from mild depression, but for a number of reasons didn't want to treat the condition with Prozac or any other drug. Despite having a good job and many friends, Tom was in a funk, unable to take much pleasure from any activity. He was functional at work, went on dates, and got together with his friends every so often, but this thirty-four-year-old stockbroker recognized that he was mired in a blue mood and hated it. Moreover, he was convinced that his moodiness had its roots in his childhood. Tom explained that nothing terrible happened when he was growing up, but his father was always away from home and traveling for work, and his mother was very involved in charitable activities. As a result,

Tom, an only child, was raised by a series of nannies. His parents were rarely around.

To escape his dark moods and honor his ambitions, Tom decided to hire a coach. At first during coaching, Tom focused on his childhood and the low-level emotional trauma he believed he suffered. All this work helped him understand himself better but had little impact on his blue mood. His coach slowly got him interested in paying more and more attention to what he wanted his life to look like in the future—including what he wanted his mood to feel like.

While this future-oriented vision work allowed Tom to picture what his life could look like, it was obviously not the complete answer to his problems and his quest. He needed to add additional approaches, and luckily his coach recommended a number of options. One of them involved working with a greater focus on dating. During these sessions concentrating on dating, the coach became aware that Tom had never been in a serious relationship for more than a month or two. Typically, Tom dated women who he acknowledged were somewhat superficial and uninterested in commitment or marriage. He began to gain insights regarding the qualities he sought—qualities that would help sustain a terrific relationship over time. Tom realized that he wanted to feel passion and experience mutual safety and commitment with a woman. With the coach's help, he learned how to describe and recognize the qualities he sought.

The coach also encouraged Tom to pursue his interest in religion and spirituality. Raised as a Catholic, Tom had fallen away from the church by the time he was in college, but he had retained an interest in different religions and had done a great deal of reading about them. When a friend invited Tom to go with him to a Unitarian church service, he went and enjoyed the experience greatly. Pretty soon he joined the congregation and became actively involved in church activities.

Over the next year, Tom also began dating a woman he met at religious services. He noticed that she possessed many of the qualities he sought in a mate. The dating soon evolved into a committed relationship and eventually led to marriage. Several years back, Tom had given up on ever meeting someone he would marry, so meeting this woman and marrying her felt like a real-life miracle.

The coach had also asked Tom to consult with a psychiatrist in town about taking medication. Tom agreed to take a very low dose of a safe and nonaddictive antidepressant medication. It seemed to help build his stress tolerance, mood, and resilience. Tom noticed that he enjoyed life more, things didn't bother him as much, and his mood was consistently brighter.

So before long, with the multifaceted interventions just de-scribed, Tom's satisfaction with life increased considerably. Progress was made because the coach was open to introducing simultane-ous or multidimensional approaches to his client. Initially, Tom had been fixated on the emotional symptoms in the sphere of Self. He viewed most of his problems as developmental in nature (the Self sphere), but his coach helped him see that he also had to address life skills in the Self sphere and in other spheres as well—Love (dating), Spirit (religion), and Body (medication), to name three—before he could start leading a happier, more satisfying life.

Though Tom was helped, encouraged, and challenged greatly by his coach, he did a lot of work on his own. You can use the spheres to address the issues that are holding you back from achieving your life goals, no matter where they occur.

In the next chapters we will introduce the concept of the three Big-spheres: You, Career, and People. The Big-spheres organize the eleven spheres into these three areas of life.

Read the next Inspiration and complete this chapter's coaching exercise, Life Investigation (in eleven parts). The following exer-cises will help you start thinking in spherical terms as well as show you some of the issues that need to be addressed in each life area. Refer to the client's sample completed exercise. Blog your thoughts in your journal or online while they are fresh in your mind.

DR. JOE'S INSPIRATION

"Eventually you will need to consider leaving therapy in the dust to pursue a fresh, multipronged approach to achieve your key ambitions."

Full Life Exercise

Life Investigation

Sphere	How Life Is Working in Sphere
Self	
Work	
Love	
Family	
Body	
Friends	
Community	
Spirit	
Money	
Fun	
Home	

Sphere	How Life Is *Not* Working in Sphere
Self	
Work	
Love	
Family	
Body	
Friends	
Community	
Spirit	
Money	
Fun	
Home	

STACY'S RESPONSE

Sphere	How Life Is Working in Sphere
Self	I am generally confident and grounded. I am organized and punctual.
Work	I enjoy my job as a copy editor. I learn a lot about topics in the articles I edit. I enjoy many of my colleagues and respect the company for which I am employed.
Love	I have been dating and am open to a relationship. I find very decent guys to date.
Family	My family is very loving. I have two great parents and three siblings to whom I am close.
Body	I generally like my body. I eat decent-quality food, and I work out once per week in the gym.
Friends	I have a group of three terrific friends from college who now live in my city.
Community	I feel part of the Greek American community. I volunteer in a soup kitchen.
Spirit	I enjoy my Greek Orthodox religion and attend services every weekend if possible.
Money	I make a decent salary at work. I am beginning to save a percentage of my salary.
Fun	I have a lot of fun on weekends going to films, theater, and restaurants.
Home	I like my studio apartment and have worked very hard on the furnishings.

Sphere	How Life Is *Not* Working in Sphere
Self	I experience a lot of social anxiety before important business functions and before meeting dates for the first time. I am often irritated with others.
Work	I am often bored at work. I don't have enough work to keep me busy.
Love	I don't seem to ever go beyond the second or third date. I have no idea why this always seems to be the case.
Family	My parents are divorced, which is very upsetting for me. I have never stopped picturing the perfect family, and I feel very sad that my family has been split apart.
Body	I had an eating disorder as an adolescent and still purge once a month after overeating.
Friends	I have not met many new people in town whom I would like as a close friend. This concerns me because I don't want to depend on college friends.
Community	I yearn for another group experience that is separate from the Greek American community.
Spirit	I don't like all the scrutiny from the other congregants in the Greek Orthodox church to which I belong. People are very judgmental that I am still single. Everybody seems to talk negatively about each other as well.
Money	I spend too much on clothes, and I don't budget well. I am always worrying about money.
Fun	I don't have enough fun on weekdays.
Home	My apartment is too small.

STACY'S BLOG

I realize that there is so much I want to see happen in my life. I am no longer satisfied with just talking about it. I want to see stuff really change and start moving forward in my life. I want to have a great relationship, I want to stop purging completely, I want to have an interesting job, and I want to manage my money better. I am not going to stop until I achieve the things I want.

CHAPTER 9

The You Spheres: Self, Body, Spirit, Fun, and Home

The You Big-sphere is all about you: encompassing the spheres of Self, Body, Spirit, Fun, and Home. It is centered on what's going on inside of you and how you derive meaning, pleasure, and sustenance from your life. Unlike the other two Big-spheres, this one is not necessarily interdependent on others. It's all about how you think, feel, play, and take care of you.

The five spheres are a much broader definition of *you* than traditional therapists would offer. Most people go to therapists for specific problems or issues: depression, anxiety/panic attacks, angst, relationship problems, and so on. With the exception of relationships—which I place in a separate sphere (Love)—all this has to do with the Self sphere. But who *you* are ranges far wider than your anxiety or personality. If you only focus on a

The *YOU* Big-Sphere

single Self issue, you may come to terms with it, but the odds are you will still have significant issues—issues that you may marginalize because therapy tends to marginalize (or ignore) them. In fact, as you'll now discover, it's crucial to work in the Self sphere with a broader perspective.

Self Sphere

This sphere is all about individual development, confidence, management of life, happiness, and satisfaction. It is about what makes you uniquely you, such as who you are as a person, your identity as a man or a woman, and your awareness of your strengths and weaknesses. It is the sphere where your feelings about living the life you want lie.

Issues in the Self sphere can involve anything from low self-esteem to anxiety to anger management issues. Procrastination and poor organization may be examined. Traditional therapy helped people understand themselves more and was especially effective at getting to the root of the problems and providing an approach that helped people identify their issues, express their feelings, and manage their thoughts. Traditional therapy, however, usually won't help you solve your problems and work toward goals throughout life. It might help you identify your negative behaviors, such as addictions and bad habits, but rarely offers effective strategies for managing these issues.

For cultural and other reasons, many people lack social confidence and believe that they are not equal to others. They sometimes are even delayed in their development because of the cultural messages they have received that they are "less than" others. They need to increase confidence, foster normal development, and decrease shame, energizing themselves to design the life they want to live.

Therapy does not usually offer people a road map for achieving these types of goals and measuring outcomes. Coaching, on the other hand, does address the Self sphere while also targeting life goals in all spheres while working toward greater resilience, momentum, and general optimized life performance.

Doug wrestled with low self-esteem his entire life. As a highly successful attorney specializing in real estate issues, he enjoyed a satisfying and financially rewarding career. Married with three kids, Doug also had a rich family life. On the surface, it would seem that he should feel proud of himself and his success in personal and professional endeavors. Doug couldn't even point to a traumatic upbringing as the source of his low self-esteem, having been raised in a loving, supportive environment. Nonetheless, Doug felt incompetent and overextended, even in his law practice—he thought he had done a good job of faking it and that any day people would see him as the fraud he really was. He doubted his skills as a husband and especially as a parent; his adolescent daughter's issues completely befuddled him.

Working with a coach, Doug began to discover that his low self-esteem was mainly expressed in the Self sphere. However, it was clearly related to his perceived lack of ability in other spheres as well. Working with a coach, Doug discovered that a lot of his self-esteem problems were rooted in the Body and Spirit spheres. Doug had been overweight all his life, and he was convinced that people viewed him as overindulgent, sloppy, and undisciplined because of his weight. Similarly, he complained of feeling empty inside. Doug felt no part of any religion, and he confided in his coach that sometimes he felt like a mercenary or a free agent— that he went about his life as if he were just going through the

motions. Doug's coach helped him articulate these Body and
Spirit sphere issues as well as his goals for optimizing them.
One goal was to lose weight, and the coach referred Doug to an
excellent weight loss clinic—Doug lost forty pounds over the next
fifteen months. In addition, the coach created a plan that allowed
Doug to explore various spiritual and religious possibilities. After
examining multiple faiths, Doug eventually became a Buddhist.
Achieving these two goals gave Doug's life a new sense of meaning and purpose. He not only felt more confident at work, he also
brought a wisdom and patience to parenting that he previously
lacked.

While Doug's story illustrates one pattern of Self issues and
goals, many different types exist. To help you become familiar
with the range of issues in this sphere and the ones you can start
addressing on your own, here are four examples:

1. Arrogance that alienates everyone, that prevents relationships from being formed, or that weakens existing relationships; a belief in one's superiority that may drive you
to success in the Work sphere but creates havoc in your
personal life; the need to manage this arrogant quality and
turn it into quiet confidence or humility.

2. Anxiety that makes you awkward or anxious in social
situations; you may have trouble speaking or being with
someone who is of romantic interest or maintaining an
equal relationship with work colleagues or friends; whatever the root of this anxiety (it often goes back to childhood or has a genetic component), you need to learn to
manage your anxiety, respect yourself, and be proud of
who you are.

3. Shyness that causes you to withdraw from people in all life
arenas and prevents you from sharing who you are with
others; shyness can be debilitating and lead to terrible
loneliness; the goal here is to understand the cause of this
shyness and create a plan that helps you take small steps
in the direction of being more open with and connected to
others.

4. Anger that is off-putting to everyone, from friends to your children; people with bad tempers can say and do things that they (and others) regret the rest of their lives; managing anger is possible, but it takes real commitment and persistence; you need to identify the common triggers for your temper and design a plan that makes sure you don't set them off—or that you know how to respond calmly to them.

Self-Survey No. 1: Question Your Self

The following questions are designed to help you determine if this is a sphere where you need to do some work. If you can answer yes to most of these questions, you probably are dealing well with issues of Self. If not, then your no answers should serve as indicators about some of the issues you need to address in this sphere.

1. Can you list five personal strengths? (Or do you find yourself stumped and able to name only two or less?)
2. Would you characterize your mood as generally neutral to good and that the lows are relatively infrequent?
3. Do you rarely become depressed, anxious, or angry? (whether medicated or not)
4. Are you generally happy with the person you are?
5. If someone you admired or envied offered to exchange lives, would you be unlikely to take him or her up on that offer?
6. Are you able to function well in most social situations?
7. Are you able to admit your mistakes and reflect on them without beating yourself up or obsessing about them?
8. Are you very organized?
9. Do you like the person you have become?
10. Do you rarely exhibit bad habits?
11. Are you confident?
12. Are you humble?

Self-Fortifier: Ways to Build Self-Confidence

People often have trouble taking action in areas related to Self because they lack self-confidence. Too often they find themselves stuck and can do no more than talk about their problems with their therapists. Here are some actions you can take to get yourself unstuck by becoming more self-confident. Start by creating a three-column table in your journal.

- First column: Identify and list the specific events or situations that cause you to lose confidence.
- Second column: Next to each item on the list, write how you feel and think when you experience these events or situations.
- Third column: To feel better about these events or situations, name actions or a new way of thinking that would boost your self-confidence in these circumstances. For instance, if you become insecure before public speaking, you might write:
  - I will stop worrying about what others think before speaking up and give my opinion without fear.
  - I will say exactly what's on my mind.
  - I will role-play my presentation with a friend beforehand.
  - I will remember that I have been successful before in many presentations.
- Choose just one item on your action list to implement in real life. Try it out in a relatively benign situation where you're not overly anxious or the consequences aren't overly significant. Test your confidence-building action and then reflect on how it makes you feel.

Body Sphere

We live in an age where at times it seems as if almost everyone is weight-conscious: either overweight, obese, on a diet, or exercising obsessively. The media create an ideal body image that few people can live up to, and we often feel hopeless or anxious if we can't conform to this image. Dealing effectively with overall wellness—body image, nutrition, and health and fitness issues—can have an enormously positive impact on other spheres, providing energy, a sense of well-being, and even longevity.

Dean was 5 feet 9 inches and weighed 275 pounds. He had developed diabetes and was worried about his health in general. Yet, when he fired his therapist and hired a coach, Dean's motivation wasn't to lose weight. Instead, he was more concerned that his career was going nowhere and that he wasn't having much fun in his life when he wasn't working. It took a number of sessions for Dean to recognize that his life plan needed to focus on weight reduction as well as making a career move and becoming involved in more enjoyable activities. Dean wasn't having much fun because he lacked the energy to do much when he came home from work; he also wasn't particularly interested in meeting other people because he was embarrassed by how he looked. In addition, Dean was a salesperson with a large corporation, and though Dean's boss appreciated his intelligence and his ability to meet existing customer needs, he was reluctant to send Dean on new client presentations because he looked unprofessional. Therefore, the coaching plan's first step was weight loss; it should come as no surprise that when Dean lost 28 pounds, he was much more eager to try new activities, and his boss was more willing to give him increased responsibility. He also began to enjoy socializing more.

Other frequently valued activities as well as some issues involving the Body sphere are discussed below:

- *Exercise.* Sometimes in cases such as Dean's, exercise isn't just about looking better but also improving your physical and mental well-being. Some coaches can refer you to personal trainers; others have backgrounds as trainers and can monitor your workouts or at least suggest a routine that would be beneficial. Other coaches can help you monitor the goals you set for completion. The good news is that there are many choices for exercise these days including sports teams, weight training, cardio training (such as running, blading, biking, rowing, stairs, skiing, and elliptical activities), and flexibility/balance/core training (yoga, Pilates, and so many other options).

- *Health and wellness.* This includes exercise (above), but this is a broad aspect of the Body sphere, including nutrition, body image, health and your relationship with primary care and other physicians, habits, grooming, meditation and spiritual pursuits, and life balance throughout the spheres. Though you certainly can do some of this on your own, coaches can help you create wellness plans as well as refer you to experts specializing in different Body sphere specialty areas.

- *Eating disorders.* This can spill over into other spheres, such as Self and Spirit, and it's a growing concern for many people in our society. Again, if this is an issue for you, you may need help from a coach or health care professionals. Nonetheless, even the world's leading expert on treating eating disorders won't be effective without his client taking responsibility for dealing with his or her problem.

Body Survey No. 1: Physical Examination

The following questions are designed to help you determine if this is a sphere where you need to do some work.

1. Start out by completing this sentence: "If I could change one thing about my body, it would be to _____ _____ ."

2. Now consider why you want to change this particular aspect of yourself. Is it because you view this physical feature as too large, too ugly, too weird? Do you have any evidence that other people find this aspect of your body off-putting?

3. Can you change this aspect of yourself through exercise, dieting, modifying your critical thoughts, cosmetic surgery, or some other method? What are the pros and the cons of doing so?

4. Assuming the pros outweigh the cons, create a step-by-step guide to help you achieve whatever change you've identified that could improve your thoughts or body. List your steps in chronological order and be very detailed.

5. Give yourself a time frame for executing this plan.

Spirit Sphere

Some people neglect this sphere because they are cynical or disbelieving about religion or spirituality, others because they are so involved in worldly activities, and still others because they haven't been able to find the spiritual vehicle that is right for them. A large subset of coaching clients come to coaching saying something like, "I am spiritual but not religious." Others say they are very happily involved in an organized religion. Everyone is so different when it comes to this sphere, for Spirit boils down to the universal themes of meaning and connection to something larger than each individual, and when this connection is absent, it makes some people sad, empty, and even miserable. As a result, they enter therapy and search for a cause in their past when the real solution is sometimes right in the here and now.

The Spirit sphere also includes the struggle of all people with self-destructive habits or addictions and how through spiritual recovery they can learn to manage these bad habits or addictions.

Alfred was brought up Catholic by very religious parents. He attended Catholic schools and hated every minute of his schooling. He found the nuns and priests to be very difficult to please, and he found the concepts of sin and hell off-putting. As a young adult, he finally was able to stop practicing as a Catholic. However, Alfred started to feel very empty, disconnected, and sad. He started going to therapy, and the therapist told him that she thought he had been traumatized by something at school. He knew this was not true. He repeatedly requested that his therapist help him discover an alternative (to Catholicism) form of worship, but she thought that religion would only provide Alfred with a Band-Aid solution to a deeper problem. Her dismissive attitude discouraged Alfred from exploring religious possibilities on his own. When he hired a coach, however, the coach created a plan to explore various religious and spiritual alternatives. The first part of the plan involved reading about these alternatives, and the next step was narrowing them down to three or four options. The third step, visiting the places of worship and meeting with someone from each group, introduced Alfred to a nearby Episcopalian congregation. Immediately, he knew this was what he had been searching for; it provided him with the sense of connection and spirituality that had been missing from his life.

If you suspect that Spirit is a sphere where you need to do some work, recognize that not everyone has the same spiritual needs. Consider the following three types of spiritual issues and think about which one might apply to you:

1. *Defining spirit.* These can be rich coaching discussions where you articulate your feelings about spirituality as well as your experiences. Through reflection and conversation, attempt to define the place Spirit may have in your life. In this way you can figure out if Spirit is what is missing from your life or if there is something else (such as relationship or meaningful work) that is really what you are missing.

2. *Exploring spiritual possibilities.* While most coaches may not have gone to divinity school or be experts at yoga or other alternative spiritual forms, they usually are tuned into the spiritual movement and can help educate you about the wide range of options. This education helps you learn about a given group or form of spirituality; and then, if you like it, incorporate it into your life goals.

3. *Fostering a more spiritual nature.* Some people aren't interested in formal participation in a religion or spiritual discipline; they are interested in becoming more spiritual
people. Coaches can provide guidance about ways to
develop this spiritual nature, from making a reflective
walk in the evening part of a daily routine, to discovering
what brings meaning to your life, to listening to music that
uplifts and inspires.

Spirit Survey: Assess Your Spirituality

The following questions are designed to help you start thinking
about how spiritual a person you've been and how spiritual a person you want to be:

1. If you were to describe a spiritual experience you had, what
   would it be? Or have you never had such an experience?

2. Do you belong to an organized religion? Does participation
   in this religion provide you with a sense of spirituality?

3. If you are disinterested in organized religion, what aspects
   of spirituality do interest you?

4. Have you ever meditated or participated in any "formal"
   exercise that fosters spirituality?

5. Have you ever felt "transcendent" or connected to a
   higher power? Has this ever happened when you've been
   in the midst of natural beauty, experiencing art, or doing
   something else?

6. Is it fair to say that you long for a spirituality of some type,
   even though you might not use those words? Have you frequently wished you could be more reflective, meditative,
   or soulful?

7. Are you happy and successful in many areas of your life
   but still feel an emptiness inside, a longing for something
   deeper, or a sense of connection?

8. Do you ever feel the impulse to pray but aren't quite sure how to do it or to whom? Do you want to believe in a higher power or consciousness, yet find yourself defeated by the cynicism of the times in which we live?

Spirit Actions: How to Take Spiritual Steps

To move from contemplating (or discussing) spiritual issues to doing something about them, take the following steps:

1. *Compare your past spiritual experiences with your current needs.* List the activities or experiences that provided you with spiritual sustenance in the past and the ones you believe might provide you with this sustenance now and in the future. Use this comparison to consider whether you simply need to return to old activities (rejoining your former place of worship) or explore new ones.

2. *Create a list of old and/or new activities and experiences that might meet your spiritual requirements.* Don't place any limitations on this list. Include everything from formal activities, such as signing up for a class in Buddhist practices, to going on a pilgrimage to a sacred place.

3. *Test one item on your list.* Take one class; go to one religious service; try meditating. This doesn't require much time or commitment, but keep an open mind and see if what you do provides at least some spiritual nourishment.

4. *Test another item on your list if the first one doesn't help.* You may have to explore a few of your options before you find the one that is right for you.

5. *Intensify the experience once you find something that resonates.* Increase your time and commitment to the activity or experience. Monitor how it impacts your life over time. Do you feel more connected and less empty? Are you able to feel like your life has become more meaningful and fulfilling?

Fun Sphere

This doesn't mean leading a hedonistic life, since that would be a life out of balance, but making sure that laughter, creativity, hobbies, adventure, and play are key components of it. There are people who may be connected spiritually but may not have cracked a smile in a year (such as a religious zealot concerned only about his relationship with a higher power). There are also those who are victims of the adage "All work and no play makes Jack a dull boy." Therapists rarely ask their patients if they're having fun, but it is a crucial question.

D. W. Winnicott (1896–1971), a pediatrician as well as an analyst in London, found that kids who were depressed or anxious did not develop normally. He found that playfulness was necessary for normal development to occur. This was a revolutionary thought, because most people tend to think of fun as a luxury, when, in actuality, it is the lifeblood of a productive and meaningful existence. If fun and pleasure aren't present, life begins to lack any luster. People often work so hard—commuting to distant jobs at the expense of family, working on weekends, rarely traveling, rarely having sex, rarely going to restaurants— that they end up going through the motions of life without joy.

Woody had been a hard worker since he was twelve years old. He consistently was an A student and also held down jobs after school. He delivered newspapers, and then started his own Internet business in high school. He rarely hung out with his friends because he was too busy with his part-time jobs. In college, this pattern continued. He finished his coursework in three years while doing research between classes and during summers. He entered medical school when he was twenty-one years old, and he became a neurosurgeon by his early thirties. He married at thirty-one. He continued to work long hours and rarely saw his wife and two small children. When he was thirty-five, his wife left him. His world was shattered. He never dreamed that anything as painful as divorce would happen to him. After the divorce, he worked with a coach to understand why his marriage ended. The coach surprised him, however, when she recommended that instead they concentrate on Woody learning to have fun outside of the Work sphere. He gradually loosened up and joined sports, civic, and travel groups. Though it didn't happen as fast as Woody had hoped, he eventually met a woman on a Colorado ski trip. Now, their relationship is good, though it hasn't progressed to the point where Woody is ready to get married. Nonetheless, Woody has learned how to have fun, how to make time for activities that don't earn him money or grow the business or result in some other tangible gain. Not only is Woody having more fun, but also he's a much more enjoyable person to be around now that he's loosened up. His relationship with his kids—who are with him for weekends and on vacations—has improved significantly. They say they feel much closer to him, and that's due in part to his willingness to forget about work and enjoy just being with his children and goofing around with them.

While coaches do work with their clients on having more fun, this is a sphere where you can do a great deal on your own. Start out by understanding two of the most common Fun sphere issues and understanding which one is more pertinent to your life:

1. *Exploring what gives you enjoyment.* You can get so wrapped up in work and family that you have few hobbies, if any, or little spare time in which to enjoy them. You need to motivate yourself to pursue these enjoyable activities and integrate them into your life. Even if your schedule is jam-packed, fun can still be had. If you know what you enjoy doing, you can always squeeze a bit of time out of that schedule to make sure you do something fun at least once a week.

2. *Addressing the obstacles to fun.* Figure out what is preventing you from taking time off for vacations, for instance, or enjoying vacations when you take them. Sometimes it's simply a matter of allowing yourself to be more playful

and finding fresh ways to have fun. Or sometimes it's strategizing with your significant other or your family regarding how to derive more enjoyment from common activities.

Fun Choices: Pick Your Fun

The following is a list of ways to have fun. Many of them might not appeal to you, but at least a few of them should. Place a check mark next to at least one that you would like to try or do more regularly:

- [ ] Playing a sport
- [ ] Traveling to/vacationing in new places
- [ ] Joining a book club
- [ ] Taking a class in an area of interest
- [ ] Returning to a former and now inactive hobby
- [ ] Going to arts events (such as symphonies, operas, museums, plays)
- [ ] Walking/hiking/camping
- [ ] Playing cards or other games
- [ ] Going out more to interesting restaurants
- [ ] Reading
- [ ] Seeing more movies
- [ ] Attending professional sports events
- [ ] Shopping for antiques or collectibles
- [ ] Taking driving trips
- [ ] Going whitewater rafting
- [ ] Visiting old friends you haven't seen for a while
- [ ] Organizing a family reunion
- [ ] Learning how to paint, play music, or acquire some other artistic skill
- [ ] Another idea? Write it down: _____

Home Sphere

This sphere may seem relatively unimportant compared to the others, but home is where the heart is in more ways than one. The environment in which people spend the majority of their lives counts for a lot. A home that isn't aesthetically pleasing, one that is too small or too large, or one in a location that feels wrong can create tremendous tension and unhappiness.

Each person needs to decide what type of home or homes he or she desires. One man might desire to live on a boat, while a newlywed couple might be thrilled to buy a town house as their first home purchase. One person may stay in his modest home for thirty years; another may move once a year with the strategy of upgrading his home's value. There is no right answer because for some, less is more—they desire fewer possessions for happiness. Another couple wishes for wealth and many possessions. The key is defining what home means to you and creating a plan to achieve it.

Blanche grew up in a very poor family in Florida. In college, she fell in love with a young man, Rick, who came from a very wealthy family. They went to visit his family's various homes throughout the country and Europe. She was astonished to find that Rick's parents were preoccupied with managing all their properties, their staff, and their errands. They never seemed to enjoy all of their amazing possessions. After observing Rick's family's relationship to their homes, Blanche pledged to only have one home to worry about in her future. Initially, this was an issue in her relationship with Rick, who felt she was judging his family. He told her that they should have a home in the city and one in the country at the very least, and that his family wealth made this affordable. But for Blanche, this diluted the concept of home. For her, two homes created more problems than they were worth: Where should they be this weekend? How could they make good friends if they were in one place only half the time? It took a while for her to communicate her sense of home to Rick, but when he understood how important it was to her, he agreed that they should focus on one home only, but Blanche did agree with Rick's request to take frequent vacations to new and exciting places.

It's surprising how many different challenges people face when it comes to home. Here are some examples of the challenges often discussed during coaching sessions:

- *Uncertainty about where to live.* The internal debate can rage around city versus country, apartment versus house, suburb versus city, or whether to design it yourself or hire a designer. It can involve big and fancy versus small and simple, or it can include staying in a familiar place or trying something new. A coach can make it easier for clients to assess their options as well as which options meet their life goals.

- *What home really means.* People need to reflect on what home means to them and how it relates to the type of life they want to live; they need to articulate their concerns about living one way (such as in an expensive house that will create a financial burden) and how a given decision about a home might affect their lifestyle. Coaches can place this discussion of home in a larger context, allowing clients to see the ramifications not only on themselves but also on the members of their family.

Home Planning: Design Your Dream Home

To define what home means to you and what you need to achieve a truly fulfilling sense of home, complete the following sentences:

1. The ideal geographical location of my home is . . .
2. I want to live in this location because . . .
3. The obstacle I face in living in this particular type of place is . . .
4. To overcome this obstacle, I would need to . . .

5. Home for me also means living in a particular type of residence, such as a . . . (condo, house, apartment).

6. In terms of the size of this home, I would like it to be . . .

7. In terms of the style of the home, I would prefer that it have . . .

8. The obstacle to living in this type of residence is . . .

9. To overcome this obstacle, I would need to . . .

10. Home for me also means living in a place where I feel . . . (safe, comfortable, relaxed, etc.).

11. The obstacle to living in a place where I experience these feelings is . . .

12. To overcome this obstacle, I would need to . . .

Enjoy the following Inspiration and then complete the One Key Change in Each Sphere of the You Big-sphere exercise. Refer to the client's sample completed exercise. Blog your thoughts in your journal or online.

DR. JOE'S INSPIRATION

"Each aspect of you is sacred, whether it be your sense of worth, your physicality, your beliefs, your right to pleasure, or the place you call home."

Full Life Exercise

One Key Change in Each Sphere of the You Big-sphere

Use this method to improve something in each sphere.

Record the desired change in each sphere as listed below and then rate how much you want to make this improvement, with 0 being the lowest motivation and 5 being the highest motivation.

Sphere	Desired Change	How Much You Want the Change
Self		0 1 2 3 4 5
Body		0 1 2 3 4 5
Spirit		0 1 2 3 4 5
Fun		0 1 2 3 4 5
Home		0 1 2 3 4 5

Total Score = _____	Total Score Code
	0–2: Very low motivation
	3–7: Low motivation
	8–13: Medium motivation
	14–18: High motivation
	19–20: Very high motivation

MAJADA'S RESPONSE

Sphere	Desired Change	How Much You Want the Change
Self	To believe I am as important as anyone else.	0 1 2 3 4 <u>5</u>
Body	Lose thirty-five pounds.	0 1 2 3 <u>4</u> 5
Spirit	Find a Sunday service I enjoy.	0 1 <u>2</u> 3 4 5
Fun	Plan a trip to Kyoto over the holidays.	0 1 2 <u>3</u> 4 5
Home	Finish the basement and set up a home office.	0 1 2 3 <u>4</u> 5

Total Score = 18   **High Motivation**

MAJADA'S BLOG

I am so pleased that I am going to achieve one key goal in each sphere of the You Big-sphere. My new achievements will bring me satisfaction and pride.

CHAPTER 10

The Career Spheres: Work and Money

It's fair to say that people spend more time obsessing about work and money today than at any time in the past. More than ever before, we define ourselves in terms of our jobs. We also have become an increasingly materialistic society, wherein what we own, where we live, and how much we make also define us. It's no wonder, then, that these spheres, in the Career Big-sphere, often unbalance people's lives.

Years ago, individuals were more accepting of their careers and less materialistic. Today, we often feel like failures if we don't have the titles or the corner offices or aren't making the money we think we should. We also expect to find meaning and satisfaction in our work, and even if we're well paid, we're miserable if we find the work boring or repetitive.

For these and other reasons, coaches now exist who focus exclusively on work or money issues. We've grouped these two

The *CAREER* Big-Sphere

together in our Career Big-sphere because they often intersect. Job salaries often impact career satisfaction, and the choice of a job or career frequently determines financial compensation.

In some instances, however, these spheres don't intersect. A Work sphere issue may revolve around finding one's true calling, for instance, and money has nothing to do with the decisions involved. Or a Money sphere issue may be related to spending too much and saving too little, and work has nothing to do with this problem.

Whether or not the two spheres intersect, you can get started on developing, understanding, and appreciating the content of each sphere that makes up the Career Big-sphere.

Work Sphere

Here the issues often involve a job (usually basic work performed for the money) versus a true career (a profession) or a higher calling (something that people feel committed to and passionate about, often connected to their sense of purpose and spirituality). There are issues of financial compensation and issues of what type of work a person finds meaningful. Tough choices are to be made in this area. All spheres are interconnected, and the Work sphere can impact the Self sphere and vice versa. For instance, many people today define themselves at least in part by what they do for a living and how successful they are, depending, of course, on how they define success.

Betty Anne worked as a waitress through high school and into her mid-twenties. Her parents didn't have money for college, and her grades weren't high enough for her to obtain financial assistance. After her senior year of high school, she got pregnant from a one-night-stand and then decided to raise her child as a single parent. Throughout her twenties she continued to work as a server and be a mom until one day she decided to take education classes in the evenings. Four years later, she received her bachelor's degree in education. Then she began her first career as a teacher—she landed a job teaching fourth graders in a public elementary school. She taught in the classroom for fifteen years. Years later, she landed the job of school principal, which was a dream come true—she had achieved her calling. Becoming principal was the ultimate embodiment of her professional vision and spiritual integration with work.

To understand the range of issues that can challenge people in this sphere, consider the following topics that often arise during coaching sessions:

- *Work-life balance.* People (often those who are very successful) find this interrelationship of work and life to be out of balance, frequently because they are working so hard; they have no personal life and seem to have lost the ability to have fun; they rationalize why they work so hard, but they also know that their workaholic tendencies are endangering their most meaningful relationships. They want to restore the balance to work and life, but they don't know how.

- *Meaningful work.* In our society, people are acutely aware of working for purpose and fulfillment. Some people may be well paid but feel as if they're just going through the work motions for money; they want a job or a career that they look forward to, that they can engage in with passion, and that provides them with a sense of meaning in the world. Making the transition from a well-paying job to one that provides purpose often requires outside help from a coach or another party.

- *On-the-job problems.* People feel they aren't being recognized for their contributions; or they clash with their bosses or others in authority; or they suspect that they don't have what it takes to handle a new job; or they believe they aren't advancing in an organization as fast as they should be. Career or executive coaches can help these individuals with these on-the-job issues.

- *Entrepreneurs also are burdened with daunting obstacles for success in a start-up company.* Coaches of all types are life-saving for the leader of a new company. The job is inherently too big for one person, so coaching plays an integral role in helping them not only optimize their performance but also strategize, implement next-step goals, and delegate effectively to others.

- *CEOs and senior management team members often exist in the "isolation of the leader."* It's more than lonely at the top; it's also constant high pressure and demanding work. The performance expectations put on people in these positions are huge, and accountability relationships with coaches are often key to their successful navigation of their company.

Work Sphere Exercise No. 1: Job Satisfaction Assessment

This exercise is designed to help you assess if your current job is the right one for you. Too often, people say to themselves and others that their jobs are fine, when it's clear to an astute observer that they are not fine at all. This survey is designed to raise awareness of how you really feel about your job.

Answer the following multiple-choice questions.

1. When I wake up to go to work on Monday morning, I am usually
   A. looking forward to the day's challenges and eager to get to work
   B. in an emotionally neutral state
   C. sometimes experiencing anxiety and a desire to remain in bed
   D. dreading the prospect of going into the office

2. My job requires me to
   A. learn new skills regularly
   B. learn new skills occasionally
   C. learn new skills infrequently
   D. use the same old skills repetitively

3. In the past five years, my level of responsibility has
   A. increased significantly
   B. increased moderately
   C. increased marginally
   D. not increased at all

4. I find the people I work with to be
   A. highly stimulating and interesting
   B. friendly and cooperative
   C. a bit dull but okay
   D. irritating and obnoxious

5. I work in a field that I find to be
   A. challenging and engaging
   B. somewhat interesting
   C. boring
   D. stupid and immoral

As you can see, the A responses signify high job satisfaction, and each successive letter represents a lower level of satisfaction. By assessing your responses in terms of these letters, you can measure how much satisfaction you derive from your current work.

Work Sphere Exercise No. 2: True Calling Assessment

The following questions are designed to help you figure out what your true calling might be and why you have not found it or pursued it. There are no right answers to these questions, but they are created to help you think more deeply about what your true calling might be and how to take steps toward it.

- Growing up and all the way through college, did you have any particular work dreams? Do you still have those dreams but dismiss them because they're not "realistic"? Do they still resonate with you today, even though you may have dismissed them?

- Do you have a hobby or some other extracurricular interest that you're far more passionate about than what you do for a living? Have you ever explored how you might translate this activity into a job or a career?

- What obstacles stand in the way of turning a passion into a career? Are you concerned about whether you can provide yourself (and your family) with sufficient income to make this career transition? Or is the obstacle related to resources—it seems overwhelming to try to make this type of transition at your stage of life?

- Can you create a business plan for your true calling? In this plan, can you identify goals, budgets, time frames, and resources necessary to make a transition to work that really excites you?

Work Sphere Exercise No. 3: Everything Would Be Great, But . . .

This exercise is designed for people who are convinced they would truly enjoy their job except for a "but" (for example, "I would love what I do, *but* my boss is always picking on me.") In other words, one or more factors diminish their enjoyment or limit their potential. The following exercise is in two parts: identifying the but and figuring out how to remove it.

Part I: Identifying the But

Review the following list of buts and place a check mark next to the one that applies to you:

☐ But my boss doesn't appreciate my work.

☐ But my boss is always chewing me out.

☐ But my boss refuses to give me the interesting assignments I request.

☐ But I don't get along with the people with whom I work.

☐ But our company had a bad year, and I'm worried about being downsized.

☐ But we're asked to do too much with too few resources.

☐ But for all the stress we're under.

☐ But for the constant travel.

☐ But the work isn't particularly interesting or challenging.

☐ But I have a client/customer who is impossible to deal with.

☐ But I don't like all the new policies and procedures.

☐ But I am not paid enough.

Part II: Removing the But

The following are options for removing buts, starting with the most simple and proceeding to the most difficult (or the ones that involve the greatest risks):

- *Request changes.* Talk to your boss or any other relevant party and make your case for changing the situation to the way you want.
- *Try to strike a compromise.* Find a middle ground between what you want to make work better and what someone else wants and see if that improves your quality of work life.
- *Create a written proposal for the changes you're seeking.* Make a compelling argument in print, and present it as you would any business presentation.
- *Ask for a transfer somewhere else in the company.* Thus you're removed from the but.
- *Find a new job with another organization.*

Money Sphere

Some people make themselves unhappy because they are obsessed with money; they upset the balance in their lives by making far more money than they need and by devoting an inordinate amount of time toward this pursuit. Other people upset the balance of the spheres because they don't make enough money or worry about it all the time. Acquiring good financial skills can help you stop worrying about money all the time and free some of your energy to focus on other priorities in your life.

Millie was always late paying her bills. Her credit rating suffered, which made it impossible for her to get a mortgage to buy a home. When she was turned down by the mortgage company, she enlisted the assistance of a coach who possessed financial expertise. Millie explained that her financial ineptitude had gotten out of hand; that it was making her feel incompetent and unable to achieve more important goals, such as achieving some stability in her life. She did a number of things with the coach's guidance that enabled her to buy a home a few years later. One, she hired a bookkeeper to pay her bills so she was never late. Two, she interviewed for higher-paying jobs and landed her ideal job as a health care administrator. Three, she reduced her spending markedly: she only bought clothes when she really needed them; she followed a monthly budget for fixed and discretionary spending; and she autodeposited a fixed amount every paycheck into retirement savings. Then, two years later, because her credit rating had improved so much, she was able to obtain a thirty-year fixed mortgage at a very favorable rate. More than that, her improved financial condition enabled her to achieve the life stability she sought, and that stability served as a foundation for Millie to pursue other life goals.

Like Millie, you can improve life in other spheres if you spend some time dealing with your money behaviors. You need to make a commitment to understanding where your money behaviors are causing you problems. Here are areas where most people struggle:

- *Spending issues.* Many individuals spend too much and get themselves in financial hot water, which in turn can place stress on relationships, cause them problems at work, and ruin their credit. People have all sorts of options for managing overspending behaviors, especially when it comes to using credit cards and going on shopping sprees.

- *Managing money behaviors.* Some people are exceedingly cheap, while others are anal-compulsive in terms of managing every penny that crosses their path, and others spend far too much, as discussed above. Extreme money behaviors are sometimes signs of deeper problems and can simply be bad habits, and people need to spot these extreme behaviors, which may be preventing them from achieving desired goals. Some like to understand the root of the behaviors, but more often than not, managing them should be the primary goal.

Money Sphere Exercise No. 1: Money Statements

The following statements communicate beliefs and behaviors about money. Review each statement, and next to it place a D (disagree) or an A (agree) and a number between 1 and 10 to signify the intensity of your disagreement or agreement (with 10 representing the most intense):

- I have always had trouble controlling my spending, especially when it comes to certain types of purchases (such as clothes, vacations, cars).
- I have been called a penny-pincher, cheap, or other negative names relative to my refusal to spend money.
- I have a split personality when it comes to buying things: I'll spend a lot on one type of purchase and refuse to spend much on another type.
- My spending behaviors have a negative impact on my life and/or my relationships (the extreme effects being bankruptcy or failed marriages, for instance).
- On a number of occasions I have bounced checks because I wasn't keeping good track of the money I had in the bank.
- I have a poor credit score, in large part because I'm late with payments.
- My financial records are a mess.

- As a result of my poor money management, I have produced negative consequences (inability to obtain a loan, for instance).
- I am satisfied with the amount of money I make annually.
- I constantly worry that I don't make enough money.
- I want to make a lot more money, but I don't know how to do so.
- I am adept at making money and expect to make even more in the future.
- My inability to make a sufficient amount of money has hurt myself and my family and prevented us from doing everything we want to do.

Pay particular attention to any D or A answers with a number of 7 or above. This can signify a particularly strong money behavior or attitude you should be aware of, even if it doesn't have negative consequences. And if it does have negative consequences, you should have top-of-mind awareness of this behavior or attitude.

Money Sphere Exercise No. 2: Moderating Extreme Behaviors

The most troubling money behaviors are those taken to extremes. Look at the following suggestions for managing and moderating your behaviors in three money categories and see which ones you can put into practice.

Spending

If you're a spendthrift, try the following:

- Experiment with spending 5 percent less the first week, 10 percent less the second week, and 15 percent less the third week until you reach a percentage you feel you can maintain.
- Define extreme or unnecessary purchases. Make a list.

- Keep a journal documenting your purchases. Place an X next to any purchase that, in retrospect, seems unnecessary or extreme. Resolve not to make the same type of purchase in the next six months.

If you're overly thrifty, try the following:

- Reverse the previous experiment and try increasing your spending by 5 percent increments weekly until you reach a percentage you feel you can maintain.
- Define allowable or necessary purchases. Make a list.
- Make a list of purchases you really wanted to make but didn't in the past year. Resolve to spend the money on at least one of them during the next two weeks.

Making Money

If you're obsessed with making more and more money, try the following:

- Create a list of all the things you're missing out on because you're spending so much time and energy focused on making money (the list might include everything from spending time with family to pursuing a hobby). Make the effort to do at least one of the things on your list, even if it results in your making less money.
- Create a reasonable target money range for yourself—a range that allows you to achieve moderate money goals, from savings to lifestyle—and resolve to spend only as much time working as befits this target.

If you're beating yourself up for making so little money and need to make more, try the following:

- Ask yourself if it is feasible to make the money you want to make in your current job. Be honest about this and whether you could make what you want to make within a reasonable time frame.

- List the actions you might take to make more money, including asking for a raise; signing up for classes to obtain a needed skill; developing a new profit center in your business; obtaining an advanced degree; transferring to a different part of the organization; changing jobs; or changing careers. Decide to take at least one of these actions.

Controlling Money

If you're obsessive about your investments and accounting for every penny you make, try the following:

- As an experiment, refuse to balance your checkbook for a week. Then ask yourself what was the worst thing that happened because of this action. Many times, people need to give themselves visible proof that the world won't come tumbling down on their heads if they moderate an obsessive (time-wasting) behavior.

- Make a conscious effort to check any of your financial portfolios/investments only once a day. See if you can check them even less frequently—maybe a few times a week—and find a comfort level with that more moderate schedule.

If you frequently bounce checks and receive late-payment notices, try the following:

- Appoint a spouse or a friend as your money monitor and have him call you regularly to ask if you've paid certain bills or balanced your checkbook. Better yet, hire a bookkeeper to pay bills or get your bank to pay some bills automatically.

- Use a computer program that reminds you to make payments; this financial alarm clock can serve as a gentle reminder to exert more control over your finances.

- Set up a system with your bank to automatically pay bills so they are never late.

Enjoy the following Inspiration and then complete the One Key Change in Each Sphere of the Career Big-sphere exercise. Refer to the client's sample completed exercise. Blog your thoughts in your journal or online.

DR. JOE'S INSPIRATION

"Your career reflects your mission as a person on this planet, while your relationship to money will reveal how you live your values in each moment of every day."

Full Life Exercise

One Key Change in Each Sphere of the Career Big-sphere

Use this method to improve something in each sphere.

Record the desired change in each sphere as listed below and then rate how much you want to make this improvement, with 0 being the lowest motivation and 5 being the highest motivation.

Sphere	Desired Change	How Much You Want the Change
Work		0 1 2 3 4 5
Money		0 1 2 3 4 5

Total Score = _____	Total Score Code
	0–2: Very low motivation
	3–4: Low motivation
	5–6: Medium motivation
	7–8: High motivation
	9–10: Very high motivation

TORRENCE'S RESPONSE

Use this method to improve something in each sphere.

Record the desired change in each sphere as listed below and then rate how much you want to make this improvement, with 0 being the lowest motivation and 5 being the highest motivation.

Sphere	Desired Change	How Much You Want the Change
Work	New job in architecture with a better boss and firm vs. where I am now.	0 1 2 3 4 <u>5</u>
Money	Hire a financial advisor to make sure I save for retirement wisely.	0 1 2 <u>3</u> 4 5

Total Score = **8**   **High Motivation**

TORRENCE'S BLOG

I am usually very loyal to the people and firm I work for, but at my present job in architecture, I don't like my boss and I don't like the firm, either. I am excited to find a new job in my field at a firm I will like better and a boss I will like.

CHAPTER 11

The People Spheres: Love, Family, Friends, and Community

The four spheres that make up the People Big-sphere keep many therapists in business, especially regarding the Love sphere. Romantic relationship problems have always brought people into therapists' offices, whether for marriage counseling or for more deeply rooted individual issues. Many times, though, therapists end up acting as referees between feuding couples and as listeners for individuals dredging up their troubled pasts and trying to find the source or assign blame for their current relationship malaise. Also, lonely people often find a therapist to be sad with, instead of working with a coach on an active dating plan and development of dating skills.

Again, therapy may help, but it often doesn't lead to a successful resolution of relationship or dating issues. What most people and

The *PEOPLE* Big-Sphere

couples need is a plan of positive changes and a coach to help them put that plan into action. You can certainly work on such a plan without a coach and set your own goals and timetable. However, because coaching is a catalyst to your achieving goals and a way to acquire life skills, you may progress much faster with such an accountability relationship. Even with a coach, though, you need to spend time and energy alone reflecting on your past relationships and thinking about the ones that will be meaningful in the future.

The other three spheres—Family, Friends, and Community— often play huge roles in how fulfilling and meaningful our lives are. People can be happily married yet feel lonely and isolated because they've neglected their neighbors, lost contact with family members, and have difficulty sustaining friendships.

More so than many of the spheres, these three allow you to do a lot of good work on your own, and I'll suggest some ways in which you can improve your relationships in all these areas. First, though, let's look at love.

Love Sphere

Should you remain single or get married? Do you want to hone your dating skills? Why can't you sustain a committed relationship? Do you need to recharge your relationship? If you've been divorced, how do you overcome your fear of making the same mistakes twice? Is your marriage or relationship one of great emotional and sexual intimacy, or is there something lacking? The questions in this sphere are numerous and complex. Here, too, the sphere cannot be looked at in isolation from the other spheres. For instance, you may have work you value greatly, but it demands an enormous time commitment that precludes any type of meaningful relationship. Is this sacrifice worth it? If so, for how long?

Sylvie married her high school sweetheart during her first year of college. Her husband, Bobby, worked in a steel mill and grew increasingly insecure and hostile toward Sylvie as she excelled in her classes. One night he drank too much and hit her during a temper tantrum. Sylvie felt devastated and ashamed and went to stay at her parents' with their newborn daughter. She quickly divorced Bobby and then went into a deep depression—missing Bobby, and realizing she was single, had a new baby, and was struggling to pay college tuition.

Sylvie hired a coach to help her develop the discipline to excel in school, pay college tuition, and learn to date well. Dating was frightening for Sylvie; she had been certain that she would never have to date again, except now she was fully aware that she needed to learn how if she was going to meet someone new.

Sylvie met Sven at a speed-dating workshop. She felt instant chemistry, usually a bad sign, but this time it was a good one. Sven was kind, a mathematics professor, single, passionate, and crazy about Sylvie! One year later, Sylvie and Sven were married. They have now been married for five years, and they both believe their marriage keeps getting better with the passage of time. The reality is that they are very compatible in terms of interests, values, and intimacy needs. There is very little conflict between them.

As you no doubt know, Love is a sphere with an almost infinite variety of issues. Sylvie's problems, though common, describe just one of many areas where you can introduce positive changes in your life. Though Sylvie had a coach's help, she also did a lot of work on her own. Here are four common romantic relationship issues that people can confront; see which one applies to you:

1. *Obsessiveness.* For instance, John is smitten with Joan. Joan eventually rejects him, but John isn't interested in seeing anyone else because he still believes Joan is the only person

for him. There is no chance of getting back together with Joan, but she is all he can think about. John needs assistance in coming to terms with the end of the relationship with Joan and learning how to move on.

2. *Loneliness.* Both single and partnered individuals feel isolated. Singles need to work on dating skills and "getting out there." Partnered people need to examine why they feel such loneliness and come up with a plan with their coach to decrease the sad feelings and reestablish connection to their mate. When the loneliness is secondary to an "incurable" relationship incompatibility, separation or another plan of action needs to be contemplated as well as discussed.

3. *Infidelity.* Some individuals seem incapable of being faithful to one partner, even though they love that partner and don't want the relationship to end. Yet, that is exactly what will happen in most relationships unless they get help; they need to be coached on whether they will work toward a shared value of monogamy, create an alternative form of a relationship, or split up—and then create a plan with that goal in mind.

4. *Renewal.* Some good relationships go stale, often because one partner has dropped the ball. She has lost interest in her partner because of the onset of middle age, health problems, or because her career problems are impacting her love life; she needs to figure out if the relationship is worth sustaining and, if so, what she needs to do to help sustain it. Often, one partner's constant judgment of the other precipitates failure of the relationship; he needs to stop criticizing her or she will leave.

Love Sphere Exercise No. 1: Patterns

Most people take a myopic view of relationships; they focus exclusively on the one they're in rather than a pattern of relationships over time. The latter can yield extremely valuable knowledge, telling you what your tendencies are in romantic relationships. To help you determine the pattern in your relationships, take the following steps:

1. Create a list of all the significant romantic relationships (not one-night stands or very brief relationships) you've had in your life through the current or most recent one.
2. Next to each person listed, describe the qualities of the person you were with by writing a few descriptive adjectives and their values.
3. Next to each person, describe what attracted you to this person (such as sense of humor, beauty, same interests).
4. Next to each person, note the point when the relationship started to go downhill and what precipitated the slide (such as their judgments, their tantrums, argument about getting married).
5. Next to each person, identify the reason the relationship ended and who ended it.
6. Review the previous five steps and look for patterns (for instance, in four of your five relationships, the relationships ended because you couldn't make a long-term commitment).
7. Reflect on what a given pattern (or patterns) says about your relationship tendencies; think about how these tendencies may be counterproductive and what behaviors you might moderate so they don't have negative effects. Remember also to reflect on all your strong and positive relationship tendencies. These are the strengths you will want to build on in the future.

Family Sphere

Family can provide both great support and great heartache. But one thing is for sure: blood relatives play a key role in most people's lives. It is said that you can pick your friends but not your family. Like it or not, your familial connections will probably endure despite disagreements and disappointments. On the surface you may feel that you have little in common with a blood relative. But often, years later you experience a new bond with that same person that feels sacred and deep.

Parents are devastated when their children are sick, rebel, or make bad choices; they have many anxieties related to their children, including Love sphere issues such as how children will react when Mom or Dad remarries. We're also finding that people are redefining family and struggling with these new definitions. What is family to you? What is a gay family? Can a family be one of close friends instead of the traditional spouse and kids? How does the relationship with the grandparents work when there is so much geographical distance involved? How is a single-parent family different from a two-parent household? How does a family survive after a divorce?

Rena grew up with a mother, a father, and a younger sister until she was in seventh grade. Then her mother informed the family that she was divorcing her husband (the father) and moving in with another man who happened to live in the same city. Rena's world felt shattered. She became depressed, and it took years for her to heal from this trauma. She could not believe that her mother would do this to the family. She went to live with her father and did not see or speak to her mother for ten years. When she was at her college graduation ceremony, her mother showed up unexpectedly. In that moment, all the years of separation and anger melted away. Rena was glad to see her mother, and the occasion marked the beginning of a much more positive relationship. Unfortunately, Rena and her mother had squandered many years. If both had seen a coach together earlier, they might have been able to repair the damage faster by coming up with a plan to work through the grief and many changes while staying connected.

Be aware that family problems come in all shapes and sizes. Nonetheless, most of them fit into the following categories:

- *Family conflicts.* Disputes between or among siblings, parents, kids, and so on; these conflicts often can simmer for years and then explode because of a stressful event, such as the death of a family member; people need to gain insight and guidance that help them resolve these conflicts or at least learn to manage them.

- *Child-raising issues.* Dealing with "problem kids," especially adolescents: part of a coach's job might be to help a client understand why teenagers act the way they do and offer some alternative do's and don'ts so parents don't make a bad situation worse. Also, many parents work with a coach to become better parents for the sake of optimization; no major problems need to be present.

- *Redefining family and dealing with this redefined entity.* As the definition of family broadens, people need to come to terms with what family means in a modern context; this can mean everything from dealing with stepparents and stepchildren to being a single parent or a gay parent or parents. Some coaches specialize in these areas and have expertise that few therapists possess, but it also helps when people bring a raised consciousness about these issues to the table. Working through fear—and acceptance—is vital in acknowledging different forms of family.

Family Sphere Exercise: Problem-Solution Options

Family issues can be enormously complex, so this exercise isn't meant to serve as the definitive approach for everyone. Nonetheless, it may help you think about the family issues you face from a fresh perspective. I've listed some of the most common family problems, followed by options for problem-solving actions. Go through the option for the particular problem you face and consider whether you might take advantage of an option:

Problem No. 1: Family feud—conflict with other family member results in disconnection.

Option No. 1: Initiate written contact—use a very positive letter or e-mail to break the ice.

Option No. 2: Arrange a breakfast, lunch, or dinner to talk about the issue in a public place (thus increasing the odds that you and the other person will be on your best behavior).

Option No. 3: Bring along a mediator to a meeting with the family member to help you both work through the issues.

Problem No. 2: Adolescent rebellion—son or daughter acting out and creating havoc in the household.

Option No. 1: Try more tolerance; loosen the discipline a bit as long as your child's behavior isn't endangering himself or others.

Option No. 2: Try more discipline; tighten the reins if you believe your child has been taking advantage of your tolerance and trying to see how much he can get away with.

Option No. 3: Use more emotional honesty and less judgment; stop telling your child that what she's doing is wrong and start telling her how you feel and think about what she's doing. Realize that your child may have different opinions.

Problem No. 3: Decreasing family bonds—less communication and emotional connection with siblings, parents, adult children, cousins.

Option No. 1: Hold regular family reunions to improve connections.

Option No. 2: Commit to using different communication tools—phone, letter, e-mail, in-person visits—to establish contact with greater frequency.

Option No. 3: Tell the disconnected family member how you feel about the growing distance (rather than ignoring the topic or talking about it in nonfeeling terms).

Friends Sphere

Some people are too focused on the Work and Family spheres, and as a result they allow old friends to fall by the wayside and fail to make new friends. Sometimes they view friendship as something that was fine when they were younger, but as a luxury in adulthood because they're so involved with work and family activities. At a certain point, however, a lack of good friends can catch up to them. Especially after a divorce, a death, personal illness, or other significant life change, the lack of true friends can be devastating. Married men are especially at risk of having few or no friends if their mates make all the friends and social plans. These men often have few friends besides their mate. Depending on their spouse for their social life makes them less interesting and vulnerable to isolation if their marriage ends for any reason.

Through the ages, philosophers have suggested that a man or a woman should be judged by the quality of their friends more than by their own deeds. The following story illustrates this adage.

Pedro was a happily married man with few male friends. He had a great marriage, three terrific kids, and a career he loved as a high school history teacher. However, when Pedro was forty-five, his wife suddenly became ill and died of a rare blood disease. Pedro devoted all his time after her death to being a father and working as a teacher, yet it wasn't enough. He wasn't interested in remarrying (at least during that first year after his wife's death), but he longed for a greater connection—with friends, the church, the community. As a result, his coaching plan focused on exploring these spheres and making a conscious effort to establish the connections previously missing from his life. The new friendships Pedro formed didn't replace his relationship with his wife, but they provided a connection with other adults that he never realized he needed when his wife was alive. His participation in his church and in community activities renewed his sense of connection to God and to others in need. But most importantly, Pedro now had friends in his life. Pedro later went on to date, but he was a much more evolved and content man when he did.

The Friends sphere tends to create more specific challenges than some of the others, including:

- *Making new friends.* Some people become isolated because of work or because they've just moved to a new city, and they have a tremendous need to make new friends; they often either make efforts in this direction and are rejected or they feel too shy to initiate friendly overtures. Many coaches can target friend-building skills and suggest tactics that facilitate the formation of new relationships that can lead to friendships. For example, civic and community groups, activity groups, volunteer organizations, and sports are all ways to regularly meet and spend time with new people.

- *Broadening groups of friends.* Some people have had the same friends all their lives and are anxious to meet different types of people; they have had the same friends since high school and are eager to establish meaningful relationships with a more heterogeneous group. You can do some research on the Internet and thereby gain access to groups and activities like those listed above that will help you achieve this goal.

Friend Sphere Exercise: Tips on How to Make Adult Friends

Many people over thirty find it difficult to make new friends, in part because they're so busy with work, family, and other activities. Here are some suggestions for initiating friendships that may seem obvious but often aren't considered or acted on:

- Join a group related to one of your interests—a book club, a health club, a bike club—and see if there are any like-minded members with whom you hit it off.
- Take an adult education class in an area of interest and see if any of your classmates are friend material.
- Reconnect with old high school or college friends with whom you've lost touch; go to reunions, search for them on the Internet, or contact them via e-mail.
- Make an effort to talk to parents of your kids' friends at events such as school functions or birthday parties.
- Make a conscious effort to think about making new friends when you go to social functions or engage in

other activities; look at people you meet as potential friends rather than simply as neighbors, other parents, or classmates.

- Take a chance and suggest getting together with a potential friend for a meal, coffee, or a sports activity.
- Reciprocate (within a few weeks) and invite a potential friend to do something if he or she has invited you to do something.
- Don't rule out people as friends just because they're older or younger than you, because they're a different gender, or because they're not like the friends you had when you were younger. You may be looking for a new type of friend you never had.

Community Sphere

In many areas, people live in a place but aren't really part of it. They don't know their neighbors, they don't participate in community activities, and they don't give back in any way. Again, our busy and transitory lifestyles contribute to this lack of community involvement, and we don't grasp that this lack of involvement can cause us to feel adrift in the world. People complain about feeling a lack of purpose in their lives, but community involvement and volunteerism can counteract this feeling.

What groups do you feel a part of? Are there any groups with which you would be open to becoming more involved? Groups can range from ethnic groups to civic groups, sports clubs, soup kitchens, food pantries, travel groups, or charitable groups. Groups are important to allow people to feel connected to others in a world where it is increasingly difficult to be part of a group experience that matters. This is why organizations such as Habitat for Humanity have been so popular—volunteers build new homes for those in need. These organizations serve as a framework for individuals to be connected to others. Connection is vital for human beings, even though at times we may be so busy that we forget this basic principle.

Max had always been preoccupied with making money. From the time he graduated from college, he was running one small business after another. Eventually he built a hugely successful IT consulting company. Computers were his life. He worked fourteen-hour days and rarely saw his wife and kids. But in his forties, he started to feel down for unknown reasons. By then he was earning a huge income. At first, making money felt great to him, but soon he discovered that it felt good for only a while. He began to consider his personal mission and value systems. He began to wonder how he could give back. He had always admired kids who came from poor families and still went on to be successful. He decided he was going to help poor kids get computers. Every year from that time forward, he bought PCs for a class of students in an underprivileged school. He also volunteered and helped teach the students how to use them. Giving back made him feel balanced and proud.

To give you a sense of how you might achieve different community-related goals, consider the following options:

- *Volunteering possibilities.* This is an area that therapists might feel is outside of their expertise but where coaches feel comfortable helping clients; you also can explore the possibilities on your own by using the Internet to look up local organizations that give back to the community, making it easier to decide how you want to contribute to your community.
- *Special-interest groups.* In most communities a variety of groups exist, ranging from gourmet food clubs to political groups.
- *Exploring the notion of community.* Sometimes people aren't even aware of their need to be part of a community; they may express that they are lonely or say they don't feel part of anything larger than themselves. People need to reflect on whether the problem is their disconnection from the people and groups right where they live.

Community Sphere Exercise: Involvement Questions

While many people complain or fret that they don't feel part of their community, it's often because they don't make the effort to be involved. Ask yourself the following questions to determine if you've made this effort:

- Do you attend at least three or four community meetings (PTA, city government, neighborhood associations) annually? If you attend these meetings, do you speak when community participation is requested? Do you volunteer when volunteers are needed for projects?

- Do you participate in events sponsored by your community such as races, walks, or bake sales?

- Do you know your neighbors, especially the ones who live closest to you? Have you made an effort to introduce yourself and get to know them? Have you invited them over for coffee? Have you attended block parties or other neighborhood functions?

- Have you ever taken on any community leadership roles? Have you ever run for alderman, served on school boards, or coached Little League?

- Do you volunteer your professional skills to help your community? Do you offer legal, medical, financial, or other skills to help city government, schools, or other groups that lack the funds but could use your expertise?

- Do you volunteer for local consumer advocacy groups that are concerned with issues such as the environment, illiteracy, or hunger?

The Spheres Quiz

Now that you have a better sense of what each of the eleven spheres entails, you might find it helpful gauging where you stand within each sphere. It's difficult to pinpoint strengths and weaknesses within a sphere, but taking the following quiz can start you thinking about these sphere issues. Then it will be easier to complete the coaching exercise at the end of this chapter. Therefore, keep in mind that this quiz is simplistic, while it serves as a jumping-off point for you to think about each sphere as it pertains to your life.

Self Sphere

1. Would you characterize your life as
   A. happy, meaningful, and satisfying
   B. pleasant but not particularly fulfilling
   C. unhappy and largely meaningless
   D. none of the above

2. Do you feel you have experienced
   A. a significant amount of growth and development over time
   B. a moderate amount of growth and development
   C. stagnation
   D. none of the above

3. When it comes to your coping skills, do you
   A. deal effectively with whatever emotional stresses come your way and remain functional
   B. struggle on occasion with anxiety and other emotions and are less functional than normal during these periods
   C. become dysfunctional when negative events occur
   D. none of the above

4. When it comes to management of tasks and time frames, do you
   A. manage very effectively
   B. manage with only moderate effectiveness
   C. manage with low levels of effectiveness
   D. do none of the above

5. Do you usually feel
   A. very confident?
   B. moderately confident
   C. insecure?
   D. none of the above

Work Sphere

1. In terms of your current job, do you find it
   A. rewarding intellectually, emotionally, and financially
   B. enjoyable but not what you want to be doing five years from now
   C. boring and stupid
   D. none of the above

2. Are you pursuing a career that is
   A. what you want or your true calling
   B. something you're good at but don't particularly like
   C. something you're not good at and don't like
   D. none of the above

Love Sphere

1. Are you in a committed relationship with someone you view as
   A. your soul mate
   B. a good companion
   C. a less than satisfactory companion
   D. none of the above

2. The following best characterizes our relationship:
   A. outstanding emotional and physical intimacy
   B. moderate intimacy and good times
   C. frequent conflict and quarrels
   D. none of the above

3. You are dating someone you view as
   A. the right match for you
   B. a decent person
   C. the wrong match for you
   D. none of the above

Family Sphere

1. Does your family provide you with
   A. continuous love and support
   B. love and support, but only at certain times and regarding certain issues
   C. heartache and arguments
   D. none of the above

2. When you are with your family, do you
   A. spend a lot of time sharing not only "news" about your lives but also emotional truths
   B. sometimes talk about things that matter and sometimes ignore sensitive issues
   C. try to get through the time together without any major blowups
   D. none of the above

3. If you have a nontraditional family, do you
   A. value it more than your biological family
   B. value it equally to your biological family
   C. value it less than your biological family
   D. none of the above

Body Sphere

1. I view my body as
   A. perfect just the way it is
   B. imperfect but tolerable
   C. a mess
   D. none of the above

2. My physical condition is
   A. excellent
   B. average
   C. poor
   D. none of the above

3. Nutritionally, I make sure I
   A. eat healthy foods
   B. do pretty well but don't pay that much attention to whether I'm eating right
   C. eat whatever I feel like and don't care if it's nutritious
   D. none of the above

4. Medically, I am
   A. in outstanding health
   B. moderately healthy with some mild conditions
   C. in poor health
   D. none of the above

Friends Sphere

1. I make good friends
   A. easily
   B. with some difficulty
   C. with great difficulty
   D. none of the above

2. When I'm with my friends, we spend most of our time
   A. talking openly and honestly about things that matter
   B. mostly focusing on what's going on in our lives but usually don't share deeply personal feelings
   C. exchanging gossip and/or talking about sports
   D. none of the above

3. I feel I have
   A. just the right amount of good friends
   B. plenty of casual friends but very few people with whom I'm really close

    C. few friends

    D. none of the above

Community Sphere

1. My level of involvement in community programs or volun-
teer groups is
   A. strong and committed
   B. moderate and inconsistent
   C. low or absent
   D. none of the above

2. I believe my community is where
   A. I am aware of what's going on and where I feel as if I
   belong
   B. I have some sense of belonging, but sometimes I feel
   out of place
   C. I sleep at night and that's it
   D. none of the above

Spirit Sphere

1. When it comes to my place in the universe, I feel
   A. connected and part of something larger than myself
   B. like I want to believe in something beyond what I can
   touch and see but not always sure if I do
   C. disconnected and alone
   D. none of the above

2. There are self-destructive habits or addictions in my life
that I am
   A. managing well
   B. sometimes managing well
   C. rarely managing well
   D. none of the above

3. I would describe myself as someone who
   A. regularly experiences moments of transcendence through prayer, meditation, walks in the woods, or other means
   B. has had brief moments of transcendence but wants more
   C. rarely if ever experiences anything approaching transcendence
   D. none of the above

4. I would describe my participation in organized religion as
   A. regular attendance at my congregation
   B. occasional attendance at my congregation
   C. never attended any congregation
   D. none of the above

Money Sphere

1. My financial skills are
   A. excellent
   B. average
   C. poor
   D. none of the above

2. Not having enough money is
   A. a rare issue in my life
   B. an occasional issue
   C. a major issue
   D. none of the above

3. In terms of making money, I
   A. do very well
   B. do reasonably well but often feel I should make more than I do
   C. do poorly, and am obsessed with how much I make
   D. none of the above

Fun Sphere

1. My ability to play, relax, and laugh is
   A. better than most
   B. good sometimes, not so good when I'm under stress or worried
   C. bad; I don't have the time to play, I'm not able to relax, and I've got too many serious things on my mind to laugh much
   D. none of the above

2. When I think about the fun times I've had in the past year, I
   A. can name many events and experiences that were a lot of fun
   B. can name a handful of events and experiences
   C. cannot think of a single one
   D. none of the above

Home Sphere

1. When I enter my home, I feel
   A. like I've entered a place that reflects who I am
   B. fine, but I can think of a number of things I'd like to change about it
   C. uncomfortable, like I'm living in someone else's place
   D. none of the above

2. If I had an unlimited budget to change my home or buy or build a new one, I would
   A. not spend much of it, since I like my home the way it is
   B. make major renovations
   C. tear the thing down and build a new one or move to a completely new place
   D. none of the above

Clearly, the A answers suggest you're doing well in a given sphere, the B answers signify that you're doing okay, and the C answers mean you're having problems. Of course, these answers need to be taken with a grain of salt. As I noted earlier, this exercise is designed to point you in the right direction, not offer definitive instructions. Everyone is different, and you possess your own particular weaknesses or strengths in a given sphere. Still, I hope the above quiz helps you reflect on each sphere (for the coaching exercise at the end of this chapter) and consider the types of goals you want to set with your coach.

How Coaching Applies a Multidimensional Approach to the Spheres

At first, it may be daunting to think in the multiple dimensions the Spheres of Life require. In reality, however, it's a process everyone can take advantage of with a little practice and knowledge. Multidimensional coaching simply requires freeing yourself from the old therapeutic definitions, labels, and limitations—and being willing to explore areas that you may never have considered exploring in the past. Through the multidimensional approach, issues can be addressed and optimal life performance can be designed and implemented.

People often talk about how a delicious, warm bowl of soup can cure whatever ails you or how you can sweat out your demons with a vigorous workout or how a jog on the beach can help you view life differently. Most of the time people say these things facetiously, but in fact those things are tremendously helpful and even healing. We need to recognize their value and learn how best to apply these multidimensional approaches to our specific weaknesses, issues, or strengths—no matter which sphere they reside in.

More importantly, most of us lack the skills or the vision necessary to address specific sphere-related issues or goals. We don't know how to date effectively, for instance, or we aren't able to see ourselves as participants in a community activity group. To carry out effective life planning, therefore, you need to develop these skills to achieve your vision of your life in each sphere. It's challenging and exciting to do so, and it requires practice and persistence. With the goal of living a multidimensional life, however, most people are willing to do whatever is necessary to achieve their vision. The first step toward one's ideal vision of their life is moving past the old and limited schools of therapy and becoming aware of and embracing new multidimensional approaches, such as coaching.

Enjoy the following Inspiration and then complete the One Key Change in Each Sphere of the People Big-sphere. Refer to the client's sample completed exercise. Blog your thoughts in your journal or online.

DR. JOE'S INSPIRATION

"If you are humble, only then will you attract a kind lover
and be sought after by family and friends; and if you dili-
gently serve your community, you will forever be granted its
membership."

Full Life Exercise

One Key Change in Each Sphere of the People Big-sphere

Use this method to improve something in each sphere.

Record the desired change in each sphere as listed below and then rate how much you want to make this improvement, with 0 being the lowest motivation and 5 being the highest motivation.

Sphere	Desired Change	How Much You Want the Change
Love		0 1 2 3 4 5
Family		0 1 2 3 4 5

Friends		0 1 2 3 4 5
Community		0 1 2 3 4 5

Total Score = _____	Total Score Code
	0–2: Very low motivation 3–7: Low motivation 8–13: Medium motivation 14–18: High motivation 19–20: Very high motivation

RICHIE'S RESPONSE

Sphere	Desired Change	How Much You Want the Change
Love	I will have one date per week.	0 1 2 3 _4_ 5
Family	I will call my parents and each of my siblings once per week.	0 1 2 _3_ 4 5
Friends	I will get together with each of my my five best friends once a month.	0 1 2 3 _4_ 5
Community	I will attend one AA meeting per week.	0 1 _2_ 3 4 5

Total Score = **13**   **Medium Motivation**

RICHIE'S BLOG

I have been putting off dating for too long. I am working with my coach, Steve, and he and I figure I can land at least one coffee date per week. I have been working on dating skills and I think I can be out there and do it!

I dread calling my family because they make me feel so guilty and that I am not doing enough for the family. Well, I am going to call once per week no matter how I feel when I speak with them. Maybe I will get the guts to tell them to stop making me feel like crap.

Months go by without my seeing my best friends. So I am committing to make plans with each of the five, once a month. I look forward to hanging with them and always enjoy life more when I do.

Steve and I agree that I need to go to one AA meeting per week. I have been thinking a lot about vodka lately, can't get it out of my mind, so I am going to one meeting per week. Steve thinks I need to hook up with a sponsor, but I am going to hold off on that one. I paid my dues with sponsors and don't want to deal with all that again.

CHAPTER 12

Laser-Precision Outcomes

Given the eleven spheres just discussed and the wide range of issues people have, coaching can help you achieve just about any type of goal. In fact, it can hone in on objectives that are highly specific: obtaining a capstone position in your career, finding a significant other who possesses certain traits, starting over in a new geographical area. In short, coaching is highly pragmatic. It is a process designed to facilitate work in one or more spheres. Like any sophisticated process, though, it works best with instructions. This chapter is designed to help you get the most from your coaching experience, offering tips and techniques that should maximize the value you derive from it.

To that end, I'll share my proprietary coaching approach and its associated tools, including Spheres of Life Coaching and the Achilles Plan, all under the auspices of the Spheres of Life Coaching Outcomes System (SOLCOS). Since coaching is a new field, coaches utilize somewhat different tools and techniques. The above methods are ones I developed over many years. I know from experience and measuring outcomes that they are effective, and I'm confident that if you work hard, they'll work for you.

As you'll discover, this coaching approach focuses on your vision with laser intensity to help you change your bad behaviors, address any issues, and work toward your goals. No judgments, interpretations, or accusations are made. Instead, you will work toward defining the vision you want to achieve and overcoming the fear of taking real steps toward it.

Truth and the Fear Factor

As you'll recall, targeted outcomes in coaching are based on *your* vision, not what the coach wants for you or how he judges what you need. I want to help you identify and clarify *your* truth. That's not always an easy goal. If you're like most people, you've spent your life censoring your authentic opinions and yearnings. You've probably assumed an identity that was convenient, lucrative, or expected of you. You became a doctor because your father was a doctor. You became inordinately shy because of a difficult adolescence. You became wealthy because your parents made it clear to you that lots of money was vital for you to be adequate. Or you make little money because a parent repeatedly told you that you would never amount to anything. Most of the time, our outward identities and behaviors result from more complex forces than those just described, but you get the idea.

If you're like these individuals, you come to see me when your "false" identity starts causing you problems. You become bored with your profession or you go through a series of bad relationships, and you become hungry—sometimes *too* hungry—for help. People come into my office and expect me to work a coaching miracle—they've heard that coaching can solve problems quickly and want one session worth of advice. Coaching does work a lot faster than therapy, but it still doesn't work overnight. If you've spent your life forging a false identity, it's going to take a bit of time before you find the identity that fits your own vision. If you are thirty-five years old, your habits and identities have formed over a long time. It will take time and hard work for your true self to emerge.

Oliver was a very creative boy, always acting out plays with other kids in the neighborhood, and he liked to draw and color. His father discouraged these activities and demanded that his son play Little League baseball and many other sports. Oliver was pressured to get outstanding grades and was encouraged to study business when he got to college. He wanted to study something creative, such as fine arts, art history, architecture, or film, but his father insisted he study business and later join him in the family-owned construction company.

In college, Oliver found he was getting more and more depressed. He hated the business coursework and yearned to study film production. He brought up his desires with his parents, but his father immediately let him know that he was expected to study business. Oliver didn't say anything at that point, but he started to meet with a career coach at his university. In these coaching sessions, for the first time it became clear to Oliver that he wanted to be a film director. He began to research film schools in the country and applied to transfer to several. In a few months he was accepted to a terrific film school in Los Angeles. Oliver spent several sessions with the career coach role-playing how he was going to tell his parents and deal with his father's disapproval and possible refusal to pay for tuition if he transferred to the school in LA. When Oliver actually spoke to his parents he was ready for his father's negative reaction. However, what he didn't expect was that his mother turned to his father and insisted that he support Oliver in his goal. His father backed down and begrudgingly agreed to support Oliver's future career plans.

Figuring out what your truth is and clarifying your vision is sacred work. It means creating an environment where aspects of your self and even your soul become courageous enough to come out of hiding. You gradually work to develop a voice to express these hidden parts of your self.

Here and in the following chapters, I provide you with questions and exercises that will help you discover your truth. Be aware, though, that when you come upon this truth, you're going to feel elated at first, and then you're going to be fearful. It's perfectly natural to be afraid of changing into that authentic identity. As unhappy as your old identity may have made you, it was at least well known or familiar to you. As your truth emerges, you get scared, and your fear comes out as some form of resistance to change. In coaching sessions, people often recoil from their new breakthroughs and awareness. They become anxious about who they might actually be and say things such as "I can't be that person" or "I don't know how to do that." Sometimes this fear is overcome quickly, but other times it takes a while, so be prepared to go through the following stages of confidently owning your new truth.

Spectrum of Stages of Verbalization of Truth

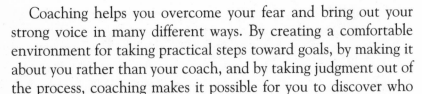

| Beginnings of Voice | Fear Response | Strong Voice |

Coaching helps you overcome your fear and bring out your strong voice in many different ways. By creating a comfortable environment for taking practical steps toward goals, by making it about you rather than your coach, and by taking judgment out of the process, coaching makes it possible for you to discover who and what you should be.

You may be in the wrong profession and now want to find your true calling; you may be involved in a bad relationship or marriage; you may be part of an organized religion that no longer satisfies your spiritual longing; or you may be a business executive who has made many ethical compromises in the past and now wants to run your company with values and integrity.

The list of possibilities is endless, and these are just a handful of examples I deal with daily as a coach. Despite the differences in how people hide from their authentic self and the distinctiveness of their personal visions, they all share a similar path on the way toward acting on these visions. As a coach, I watch how people almost always become excited when they start to realize who they are, what they can be, and how they become extremely anxious as they start moving forward. Here is an example that illustrates this dynamic.

Robert first came to see me because he worked in his family's business. He never got along with his parents, and he hated his job. Nonetheless, he stuck with his job for years, convinced that he had an obligation to his family. He rationalized this decision six ways to Sunday, telling himself that he was lucky to have a secure job that provided good financial compensation; that he would like the job more in time, especially when his father retired; and that he was good at the business and it made sense to utilize his talents. During Robert's initial sessions, he expressed these rationalizations, but as we talked about future goals, Robert kept returning to his desire to be a dentist. He had volunteered in a free dental clinic in school and received praise for this activity; one professor in college had even recommended that he pursue dentistry as a profession. Robert, though, dismissed this possibility as a pipe dream and entered the family business right after graduation. But as we spoke, Robert admitted in hindsight that he should have followed his professor's recommendation. "It's too late now," he told me. I asked him why he felt that way, and he explained that he was too old—Robert was thirty-five. I suggested that we do some research to see if we could find other people who started their dental careers later in life, and a telephone call to the admissions department of a dental school revealed that there were many dental students who began their careers after doing something else for five, ten, or even fifteen years. Then we talked about what steps he might need to take to pursue dentistry in terms of coursework, the application process, tuition, making a break from the family business, and supporting himself financially.

When Robert realized it was doable, he was enormously excited. Creating a plan for turning this dream into reality was euphoric. But this euphoria faded as we talked about the action steps he had to take. He was especially anxious about the conversation he would have to have with his father, a highly intimidating figure throughout Robert's life. On more than one occasion, Robert told me he couldn't do it, that his leaving the business would break his father's heart. It was only when we worked out a plan to transition Robert out of the business—he would remain in the business for a year while he took pre-dental classes at night—that he saw how he could slowly prepare his father for his eventual departure. Robert followed the plan we created, and now, two years after Robert first came to see me, he is enrolled in dental school and getting excellent grades. He's left the family business now and is a full-time student; he's moving toward his goal and finds life much more fulfilling than it ever was in the past.

Strengths and Weaknesses: Identify and Address Both

Do you know what your strengths are? Even if you've been in therapy for years, you may lack this awareness. You may only be dimly aware of a few things you're good at—as an accountant, you're good with numbers, for instance—but you probably possess a variety of additional strengths that apply to your personal and professional existence. In coaching, you become aware of these strengths and learn how to use them to achieve your life goals. When strengths are used properly and continuously, they can help you

- break through your fears
- turn your truth into your vision of the future
- turn your vision into Big Goals and *incremental* next-step goals
- achieve targeted life outcomes

Strengths consist of many different qualities and achievements related to all eleven spheres; they can be a characteristic you possess as well as something you've accomplished or built. The following list provides a sense of some of these strengths, but it is far from all-inclusive:

- Confidence
- Emotional well-being
- Solid and clear values
- Organizing skills
- A job you love
- A lucrative career
- Attractiveness
- A terrific relationship
- Good health
- Dating and other relationship-building skills
- A close family
- Physically and emotionally healthy kids
- Taking good care of your body
- Great circle of friends
- Sexual competence
- Strong community involvements
- Active in charity work
- Active in personal faith or organized religion
- Involved in 12-step recovery
- Solid finances
- Ability to have fun
- Great home
- A spiritual connection

Just as these strengths can serve you well in achieving your life goals, so can awareness of your weaknesses. Specifically, you need to figure out why a particular weakness is preventing you from achieving goals or leading the life you want, and explore different ways of addressing what is holding you back (the next chapter will explore the Achilles factors and how they can help you identify and confront your weaknesses). Then you can transform the weakness into a strength. This transformation can be understood within the context of opposites. For example, it is often said that a strong man cannot really be strong if he is not comfortable with his weakness. An intelligent woman cannot feel intelligent until she is at peace with what she doesn't do well. The *Tao Te Ching* is an ancient book that provides insight into the meaning and importance of opposites. Too often, people labor to understand what's wrong with themselves and see it as an unalterable condition. Coaching helps people understand their weakness, how it is holding them back, and why it's crucial for them to do something about this weakness. If, for instance, you're shy in social situations and have trouble meeting people, you need to make a conscious effort to talk to others when you're at parties, bars, and other gatherings. You could also get coaching in speaking and communication. Therefore, more than making an effort, you need a plan, tactics, and a goal to guide your efforts. This is what coaching provides. During my coaching career, I've seen people transform the following weaknesses into their opposites:

- Insecurity → Security
- Anxiety → Calm
- Worry → Peace
- Disorganization → Organization
- Unemployment → Employment
- Loneliness → Contentment
- Poor marriage → Great marriage
- Chaotic family relations → Serene family relations
- Poor body image → Positive body image
- Inadequate nutrition → Adequate nutrition
- Lack of exercise → Right amount of exercise
- Few friends → Several close friends
- No community involvement → Major community involvement
- No charity work → Charity work
- No spiritual life → Connection to a higher power

- Poor financial management → Good financial management
- Stick-in-the-mud → Has fun
- Unkempt → Neat home

Jasmine was constantly trying to control her family. She constantly criticized her husband for being a slob, for not making enough money, and for not taking care of himself. She also frequently yelled at her two kids about such things as cleaning up, bathing, and being quiet. One day, her husband let her know that he had had enough. He no longer wanted to live with someone who was so controlling and so critical. He wished she was busier or worked outside the home so she wouldn't be so difficult inside the home. At first Jasmine was really hurt, but then after thinking about her husband's words, she realized he was right, that she was becoming someone she didn't want to be. So she started working with a coach on what would be a good career for her, while also being the mother of young children.

With the help of her coach, Jasmine decided on an event-planning business. She loved to plan all the details of a party, and this career choice allowed her to be as controlling as she could muster! As she got more involved with her new business, both she and her husband noticed that she was far less controlling at home. Often she was so tired when she came home that she was loving and gentle with her husband and kids, even if there were toys left out and dishes in the sink. She didn't like it, but it didn't bother her as much. She was happy about her new career and kinder at home.

Establish Your Vision

Once you're aware of your strengths and weaknesses, you're in a good position to make changes in your life. Part of this process of change through coaching involves homework assignments where you begin to express in words and graphic pictures what you want your future to look like. You examine your value system. You investigate your mission in life and what brings you meaning and purpose. The following questions will help you visualize what you hope to achieve in the coming years:

1. What do you want your life to look like in five years in all spheres?
2. How hard are you willing to work to make this happen?
3. What are you willing to sacrifice to make this happen?
4. How will you feel if you fail to accomplish your vision?
5. How will you feel if you implement your vision?

Talking about these questions with a coach will help you clarify your vision in all eleven spheres. Typically, you'll go through the following three stages as you bring this vision to life:

Spectrum of Stages to Establish Vision

Vision Verbalization   Vision Picture   Vision Clarification

After verbalizing your vision, you create a graphic representation of it (such as in a drawing, photo, or collage). This then leads to a final description of your vision, which you can refer to as an inspiration while implementing the vision of your life.

Victoria was working as a nurse in an intensive-care unit. She was good at her work and well respected by most of her colleagues. Recently she noticed that she had been scrutinizing the physicians who came through the unit. She started to get annoyed with them when they gave her orders for a patient's care. Once she got very angry at a physician, and her supervisor reprimanded her. She was concerned because anger wasn't usually a big issue for her.

Victoria engaged the services of a coach, ostensibly to work on her anger issues. But what was uncovered in the coaching was that her anger was not the main issue—instead, it was that Victoria wanted to be a physician and not a nurse. Her anger at the physicians was just displaced. She was really angry at herself for not being a physician. Once it became clear what her Work sphere vision looked like, her pleasant rapport with the physicians returned, and she worked with her coach on making her vision of becoming a physician a reality. She began to develop her plan of incremental next-step goals as part of the Achilles Plan discussed below.

The Achilles Plan: Generate Incremental Next-Step Goals

On paper, all this may seem simple. In real life, it can get messy. As a coach who has seen almost all clients struggle at times, I know that many obstacles can stand in the way of achieving life visions. Some of these are external (such as you can't get a job that is necessary to achieving your vision), and some are internal (such as self-imposed limits on what you can achieve; fear of success; fear of change; or inadequate finances). To clear these obstacles, the Achilles Plan comes in handy.

Using the Achilles Plan, you can:

1. clarify your specific goals in each sphere;
2. establish each overall goal as a "Big Goal" with a time frame for completion (for a finite task), or as an ongoing goal (for a repeated task);
3. set incremental next-step goals to achieve each Big Goal.

In the Achilles Plan you set Big Goals in each sphere that will help you implement your vision of your life. In preparation for each coaching session, you work on at least three incremental next-step goals that work toward your achieving each Big Goal. This coaching exercise is called Achilles Plan—Big Goals and is included at the end of this chapter.

Too often, people set overly ambitious goals and become frustrated when they can't achieve them quickly or easily. By setting smaller, more reasonable goals on the way to the Big Goal, you keep yourself moving forward. These Big Goals are an integral part of the coaching process, offering people the outcomes necessary to stick with a plan (rather than quit in frustration, as often happens in therapy).

Jessica was working as an administrative assistant in a real estate office. She was tired of her job and had decided to become a schoolteacher. However, she found that she stopped making any progress in working toward a teaching career. She procrastinated and realized she was terrified of failure. So Jessica engaged the services of a coach who specialized in career transitions. She started to define her Big Goals, which included completing required coursework; investigating graduate teaching programs; investigating financial assistance; obtaining, filling out, and submitting applications; getting accepted to graduate school; and attending graduate school. Under each Big Goal, Jessica set three incremental next-step goals. With the help of her coach, she completed her goals to make the main goal happen. She found that when held accountable by her coach, she broke through her resistance and fears and was on the road to her new career.

High-Energy Outcomes: Achieving Breakthrough Big Goals

While it's important to aim for and celebrate small steps forward, it's equally important to have breakthrough Big Goals. There is tremendous value in identifying these breakthroughs when they occur and then using them to inspire and encourage people to keep moving forward with additional goals. I call this coaching exercise Cementing Outcomes (see the end of chapter 15). Many times, people downplay breakthroughs. They achieve them and then forget the accomplishment and start worrying about a new, unmet goal. Identifying these breakthroughs helps clients internalize the progress. For instance, Avery was a man in his forties who spent years lonely and dateless. After engaging the services of a dating coach, he started dating and within two months was involved in a serious relationship. By recognizing and celebrating this major achievement, Avery gained confidence that spilled over to goals in other spheres. Formal recognition and celebration are things that coaches facilitate, making sure people don't ignore or minimize what is actually a huge accomplishment.

The Cementing Outcomes exercise helps clients name and list their accomplishments. They think about how each outcome achieved changes the way they see themselves thereafter.

While major outcomes vary from individual to individual, here are examples of common breakthroughs in each sphere:

Self → Confidence rises

Love → Dating once a week

Work → Doubled revenues in past month

Family → Sister visits for first time

Body → Lost twenty pounds and exercising

Friends → Number of friends has increased

Community → Volunteering in a soup kitchen

Spirit → Found a church to attend

Money → Practices targeted shopping (must know what you will buy in advance)

Fun → Travel for first time outside the United States

Home → Major remodeling completed

As clients have discovered, coaching is an ongoing process, one that serves you well even after you've achieved a major life goal. Unlike therapy, you can stop seeing a coach for a while, return to coaching when you need it, and not lose a step. You don't have to spend weeks or months getting your therapist up to speed and rehashing old issues. A coach is outcome-focused, and this focus serves both the immediate and long-term needs of clients. As a result, the coaching process invigorates people as they move toward goals. In fact, it's why I have the privilege of witnessing the high-energy states that coaching helps release in people, and I call the overall method the Spheres of Life Coaching Outcomes System (SOLCOS).

To help you keep SOLCOS and its components—Spheres of Life Coaching, your Vision of your life, the Achilles Plan, and High-Energy Outcomes—all clear in your mind, refer to the following graphic representation:

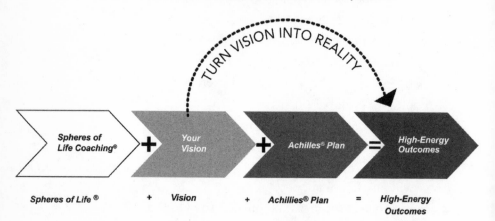

Spheres of Life® Coaching Outcomes System

Full Life Coaching takes you through an outcomes-oriented process to achieve the life you want.

TURN VISION INTO REALITY

Spheres of Life Coaching® **+** Your Vision **+** Achilles® Plan **⇒** High-Energy Outcomes

Spheres of Life ®   +   Vision   +   Achillies® Plan   =   High-Energy Outcomes

Step 1
Your issues and strengths are identified according to Spheres of Life Coaching.

Step 2
You articulate your Vision for success.

Step 3
You develop a step-by-step Achilles Plan for transforming your vision into reality.

Step 4
You work step-by-step to achieve High-Energy Outcomes in your life.

Coaching Results

Follow-up Steps

After you've achieved breakthrough Big Goals in all or some spheres, you need to follow up with activities that will maintain your achieved High-Energy Outcomes. Too often, people achieve an outcome but then slip back into old, counterproductive behaviors. Follow-up examination enables you to maintain your gains and continue to solidify your past outcomes. Another problem is that sometimes when time goes by, the former breakthrough goals no longer fit for the client and have to be revised.

For example, a client named Buffy was thrilled to run the restaurant in a very successful Los Angeles hotel. It was a major accomplishment for her, one she had worked hard to achieve. She had been in coaching for two years prior to getting the job, and it had been a struggle at first for Buffy to believe that she was even capable of running a restaurant. Two years into the job, though, Buffy began being bored. She didn't acknowledge this boredom to herself. After all, she had a great job that she had worked hard to obtain. She knew that she had lost some enthusiasm and energy, and there were times when she took shortcuts to get things done at work. Still, she was doing fine.

Then she returned to see her coach, whom she had stopped working with by mutual agreement shortly after she had secured her restaurant job. He had Buffy measure her job and career goals, and he asked her some probing questions about her work experience. Then he pulled out the goals and responses to the same questions Buffy had provided three years earlier. It was clear that things had changed. Before, Buffy said she derived great satisfaction from being in the restaurant environment—she relished the challenges of juggling all the balls that restaurant management required. Now Buffy admitted that there was less challenge in the juggling, that at times she felt she could do her job in her sleep. Buffy also mentioned that her restaurant experience had exposed her to the hotel management business because her restaurant was located in a major hotel. By talking with the hotel management staff and observing what they did, she found herself intrigued by the hotel business.

But Buffy never considered hotel management as a career until she talked with her coach and began discussing new goals she wanted to set up for herself. It quickly became clear that her goals had shifted and that her larger breakthrough goals needed to be revised to target the hotel rather than the restaurant business. While this seems obvious in hindsight, before Buffy saw her coach, it was anything but. Many times we become so enmeshed with our daily routines that we lose sight of what's important. By formally following up and considering what goals were important to her, Buffy discovered that she needed to make some changes if she were going to lead a fulfilling and purposeful life. For this reason, she quit her job, enrolled in hotel management school, and eventually secured a job with a major hotel chain.

Read the next Inspiration and complete the chapter's coaching exercise, Achilles Plan—Big Goals. Refer to the client's sample completed exercise. Blog your thoughts in your journal or online.

DR. JOE'S INSPIRATION

"Joy comes from struggling to take each step and seeing success in each little and big accomplishment."

Full Life Exercise

Achilles Plan—Big Goals

Sphere	Big Goal	Due Date	Done	Next-Step Goals
Self		/ / ☐ Ongoing	☐ ☐ ☐	
Work		/ / ☐ Ongoing	☐ ☐ ☐	
Love		/ / ☐ Ongoing	☐ ☐ ☐	
Family		/ / ☐ Ongoing	☐ ☐ ☐	
Body		/ / ☐ Ongoing	☐ ☐ ☐	
Friends		/ / ☐ Ongoing	☐ ☐ ☐	
Community		/ / ☐ Ongoing	☐ ☐ ☐	
Spirit		/ / ☐ Ongoing	☐ ☐ ☐	
Money		/ / ☐ Ongoing	☐ ☐ ☐	
Fun		/ / ☐ Ongoing	☐ ☐ ☐	
Home		/ / ☐ Ongoing	☐ ☐ ☐	

FLOR'S RESPONSE

Sphere	Big Goal	Due Date	Done	Next-Step Goals
Self	Increase confidence	/ / ☒ Ongoing	☐ ☐ ☐	Work with coach to plan ways of feeling more confident Plan activities at which I can feel competent Manage my self-critical thoughts
Work	Get more organized at work	03/01/09 ☐ Ongoing	☐ ☐ ☐	Organize desk Purge files Prepare to-do list nightly for next day
Love	Go on regular dates	04/01/09 ☐ Ongoing	☐ ☐ ☐	Discuss dating strategies with coach Write a profile on dating Web site Join a singles' hiking group for spring
Family	Be in more regular contact with folks	/ / ☒ Ongoing	☐ ☐ ☐	Visit folks once every six months Call them every Sunday Send letters/cards at major holidays
Body	Go to gym regularly	/ / ☒ Ongoing	☐ ☐ ☐	Join a gym in next week Go to gym four times per week Hire a personal trainer for two weeks to learn basics and then work out alone
Friends	Make plans with a friend once per week	/ / ☒ Ongoing	☐ ☐ ☐	Make plans for dinner Make plans for sports events Make plans for working out together

FLOR'S RESPONSE

Sphere	Big Goal	Due Date	Done	Next-Step Goals
Community	Volunteer twice per month	/ / ☒ Ongoing	☐ ☐ ☐	Volunteer for Habitat for Humanity Volunteer for breast cancer foundation Volunteer at food pantry for those in need
Spirit	Choose a church to join	/ / ☒ Ongoing	☐ ☐ ☐	Visit a different church every Sunday Narrow down to three finalists and attend each for second time Choose congregation to join
Money	Decrease shopping for clothes	/ / ☒ Ongoing	☐ ☐ ☐	Create monthly budget for shopping New rule: can only shop for what you set out to buy; no other purchases Reward self if stay within budget
Fun	Have more fun	/ / ☒ Ongoing	☐ ☐ ☐	Plan fun activity alone Plan fun activity with another Participate in new or old hobby
Home	Redecorate home	06/01/09 ☐ Ongoing	☐ ☐ ☐	Have walls painted Buy new sofa Get new carpeting

FLOR'S BLOG

I am very excited about my Big Goals. I hope to have more confidence and get more organized at work. This will be great! It is time I date again. I got really burned last time around, and I want to learn how to date better and give it another shot. I want to be a better daughter to my folks, and I want to work out better and more consistently. I want to see my friends more instead of isolating myself so much in the evenings with my flatscreen TV or book. I want to volunteer to help others and join a church. I am tired of buying clothes I don't need. I need to have more fun in life, and it is time to reinvigorate my home with a few new things.

CHAPTER 13

Overcome Obstacles to Achieve Outcomes

Sometimes we ask a lot of ourselves, and sometimes we ask too little. When you hire a coach, you are asking a lot of yourself. You're setting ambitious goals and striving for greatness. When you ask a lot, you also can expect that the road won't always be smooth and clear. Sometimes roadblocks get in the way of your goals. As we discussed in chapter 3, these obstacles can be fear, bad habits, and many other things.

Here, though, I want to focus on the obstacles hidden inside all of us, the aspects of ourselves that can cause us to sabotage our progress (unconsciously, in most instances) as we try to achieve our goals. I refer to these hidden obstacles as Achilles factors. As the name suggests, these factors describe the vulnerable heels we all possess. It may be an addictive behavior, a difficulty committing to a relationship, or issues with money (such as spending it as soon as you get it). Whatever it is, it can cause us to fall short of our life goals unless we become aware of it and address it. And, of course, that's what the coaching process should do.

While Achilles factors can trip you up, they also can be gifts that emerge from the coaching relationship. Coaching is an inexact science, and it's sometimes difficult to drill down and uncover the keys to someone's story. When an Achilles factor emerges, it can be used by the coach and client as a "hypothesis"—a starting point to interpret how this factor has influenced behaviors and explains aspects of who a person is. Notice that I did not call it an "interpretation," a term used by analysts and therapists that results in a top-down statement of fact dictated to the client. In therapy, the interpretation is often used to categorize and pathologize. A hypothesis, on the other hand, is a likely possibility that needs to be further tested by the coach and client for validity. Viewed in this manner, these Achilles factors are dynamic tools that provide insights about why people have trouble achieving their goals.

Examples of Achilles factors
- History of abuse: can be emotional, physical, or sexual
- Shame issues regarding minority status: can be racial minority, sexual orientation, or nationality
- Fear (change, intimacy, getting hurt, working harder, unfamiliar)
- Low confidence
- Self-critical thoughts
- Emotional symptoms such as anxiety or depression
- Chaotic family background
- Bad habits and addictions
- Disability such as dyslexia or attention deficit disorder
- Financial challenges
- Loneliness
- Unkind behavior to others
- Judgmental nature

Assess Your Weaknesses with Honesty

As you looked at the bullet points in the previous section, did some of them resonate with you? Or did you find yourself denying that any of them pertained to your behaviors or got in the way of your goals? The latter reaction is common. Some people have a tendency to assume a pose of invulnerability. Others rationalize their weaknesses, telling themselves that they don't have the power to impact their larger goals.

During the coaching process, you need to be brutally honest with yourself—and your coach—about these vulnerabilities. If you're not, they're going to block your progress toward your targeted outcomes. To facilitate this honesty, I've prepared a series of questions relating to each of the weaknesses previously listed. Use these questions to think long and hard about each of them. In this way you can enter into coaching with your eyes open about the deep-seated feelings, attitudes, and behaviors that may be holding you back.

History of Abuse: Can Be Emotional, Physical, or Sexual

- Do you remember being abused as a child?
- Do you suspect that you were abused but have repressed the memory or discounted it?
- Do you refuse to view the abuse as a weakness because you needed to be strong to survive it? Is your attitude that this was something that happened long ago and that you're not going to wallow in self-pity or be bogged down by bad memories?

Shame Issues Regarding Minority Status: Can Be Racial Minority, Sexual Orientation, or Nationality

- Do you ever feel embarrassed or uncomfortable because of your race, sexual orientation, or nationality?

- Are there times where you experience the paradoxical feeling of being proud of who you are but also ashamed of it?
- Do you ever try to cover up or compensate for your race, sexual orientation, or nationality?

Fear (Change, Intimacy, Getting Hurt, Working Harder, Unfamiliar)

- Are you often anxious or fearful when change occurs in your personal or professional life?
- Do you find yourself unable to engage in a committed relationship? Do you back away when things start to get serious?
- Are you convinced that you'll be hurt if you try something new or different?
- Do you usually avoid situations or experiences that are not part of your routine?

Low Confidence

- Do you often feel uncertain of your ideas and opinions?
- Are you reluctant to express yourself at work or in your personal life because you doubt that what you have to say is of value?
- Are you unable to ask people out on dates because you assume they'll say no?
- Do you doubt your ability to be effective in some area of your life?

Self-Critical Thoughts

- Do you often hear a nagging voice inside your head telling you what you're doing wrong or what you could have done better?
- Do you beat yourself up unmercifully when you make a mistake?
- Are you never satisfied with how you perform at work, no matter how well others tell you that you've done? Is this similar to your attitude toward grades when you were in school?

Emotional Symptoms Such as Anxiety or Depression

- In most instances, do you find it difficult to enjoy your life?
- Are you often worried? Do you find it difficult to relax because your mind is going a mile a minute?
- Do you feel unhappy or sad much of the time, often for no specific reason?

Chaotic Family Background

- Is your family of origin one you would characterize as highly combative or argumentative?
- When you were growing up, did your family move around a great deal?
- Did your parents have loud, sometimes scary arguments a lot of the time when you were young?
- Would you characterize your family as dysfunctional? Were your parents or siblings often in trouble, running away from home or unavailable emotionally?

Bad Habits and Addictions

- Are you addicted to things such as drugs, alcohol, or gambling?
- If you don't believe you're addicted, do you tend to become mired in certain routines that you can't escape from?
- Do you frequently have to turn down requests or avoid certain behaviors because they would disrupt your routine?

Disability Such as Dyslexia or Attention Deficit Disorder

- Do you have any diagnosed learning disabilities or other similar problems that prevent you from doing the type of work you want or enjoying a fulfilling relationship?
- If you have not been diagnosed with any of these disorders, do you find yourself disabled in certain ways in specific areas of your life? Does this disability form a behavioral pattern?

Financial Challenges

- Are you constantly in financial trouble? Do these problems prevent you from making a relationship commitment or pursuing the career you want?
- Do you feel as if you'll always be poor or just scraping by? Do you agonize about how you won't have enough to send your kids to college, buy a nice house, or retire?
- Do money issues dominate your thinking and conversations?

Loneliness

- Do you feel isolated and disconnected from people?
- Is this isolation preventing you from enjoying life to its fullest?
- Are you not motivated to achieve things in your life because you don't have anyone to share them with?

Unkind Behavior to Others

- Do you treat other people with indifference or even cruelty? Is this a common pattern in either your personal or professional life?
- Do you find that you need to put other people down to feel good about yourself?
- Would other people characterize you as a bully?
- Do you find that your unkindness prevents you from establishing the type of relationships you want, advancing in your career, or just being able to have fun?

Judgmental Nature

- Do you tend to form opinions about other people based on one incident or first impressions?
- Do you cut people out of your life frequently?
- Are you intolerant of even small, negative behaviors such as rudeness, crudity, or abruptness?

- If you are judgmental, do you find that it has caused you significant problems at work, or with your friends and family, in terms of enjoying your life?

As you reflect on these questions, you may find that you can quickly identify one or more weaknesses. That's terrific. If you're still struggling with the identification process, you should find some examples of common weaknesses helpful.

Four Examples of Achilles Factors

In coaching, what often happens is that you and your coach gradually see your Achilles factors because you become stuck on some of your goals. I'm going to tell you four quick stories of people I've coached and the obstacles they faced while achieving their goals. Then, in the next section, I'll show you how uncovering their Achilles factors and managing them helped these people make great progress toward their goals.

I was coaching Randi on improving her dating skills. She joined some coed sports teams and activity groups and visited an online Web site to meet men. However, in coaching it became clear that she was not trying very hard to meet anyone. She said she wanted to date, but her behavior said otherwise.

Valencia worked in a large consulting corporation for ten years. She had ambitions of being a partner one day, but she was constantly being told in her performance evaluations that she wasn't a strong enough leader. In fact, she was consciously trying to break the glass ceiling for women at work but found that whenever she was challenged, she seemed to sabotage herself by getting tearful in public—just at the time she wanted to appear confident.

Monty is a gay man who is working in road construction. He had hoped to be a team leader in the field, but the word spread that he was gay. Monty was a big, muscular guy and yet was constantly put down by those he worked with, usually behind his back. His manager told him that he would probably never get promoted. Monty started getting anxious and depressed; he couldn't sleep, and his confidence took a nosedive.

Laney's mother always told her that she wasn't smart or pretty and generally made the type of parenting mistakes that contributed to Laney's low self-esteem. Laney settled for a low-paying administrative job in an accounting firm with no room for advancement. In coaching, she started to work on a career plan to become a nurse. She had wanted to be a nurse for as far back as she could remember. However, soon she and her coach noticed that she was not taking the incremental next steps to become a nurse—she was not registering for the exams she had to take.

Create Hypotheses for Understanding

You and your coach need to form a hypothesis regarding how an Achilles factor formed in the first place. Understanding the factor is used to help blocked clients return to their goals and move toward breakthrough High-Energy Outcomes (in SOLCOS).

In discussions with her coach, Randi discovered that she was quite ambivalent about dating and about men. Her father had abandoned the family when Randi was young, and though she acted initially as if she were past that, it clearly had a profound effect on her. All through her childhood she heard her mother complain about how irresponsible her father was and how men cannot be trusted. So the Achilles factor Randi discovered was that she had this old tape in her mind replaying negative messages about her father specifically and all men by implication. Why would she want to date? It was only when she saw how this tape had made her vulnerable in the area of relationships that she could confront it, raise it to the level of consciousness, and create a plan to overcome this childhood-based obstacle.

In her coaching sessions, Valencia recalled that her father was always telling her to get married and not worry about a career. "Real women aren't ambitious," he used to say. Valencia's mother was a homemaker. So, the Achilles factor Valencia discovered was that she was programmed to be a homemaker and not a successful businesswoman. With her public tears, she ended up indirectly finding a way to confirm her father's belief in a woman's role, even though she didn't subscribe to it. It was only when she saw how powerful an influence her father's belief was that she could focus on specific actions that would counteract it.

Monty discovered that his shame about being gay prevented him from defending himself from the bigotry he was experiencing at work. In coaching, Monty also remembered that his father had always put him down for not dating girls. No matter how physically strong he became or the fact that he had a traditional male job—neither earned Monty his father's approval. The men at work making fun of him and putting him down were replicating the messages he had received from his father and also from his church's teachings. It was liberating for Monty to grasp why he was unable to move into a leadership position at work. Before this understanding, Monty worried that he "didn't have what it took" to become a leader. With it, he saw how something that had happened years ago was holding him back. More importantly, he was able to form a plan to do something about it—the plan dealt with the negative comments of his coworkers and provided avenues for Monty to communicate and demonstrate his leadership abilities in different ways.

Laney's initial coaching sessions involved an investigation into negative messages from her mother regarding her worth and intelligence. She realized that not pursuing her nursing education was a passive agreement with all the negativity she received when she was young. As a result, her coaching plan focused on taking incremental steps toward her nursing degree and not allowing a negative comment from a teacher or a bad grade to throw her back into her childhood mind-set.

I've deliberately chosen these examples because they demonstrate how one's family of origin strongly influences behavior later in adult life and creates Achilles factors. Be aware, though, that these factors can emerge from other experiences as well—any sort of emotional or physical trauma at any age, for instance.

Now let's talk about how these four individuals learned to test their Achilles-related hypotheses.

Test Each Hypothesis and Transform Vulnerability into Power

Testing your hypothesis about where the Achilles factor comes from involves identifying themes. When themes resurface in coaching discussions, the odds are that they relate to an Achilles factor and that they are valid reasons why you're doing what you're doing. Let's look at how Randi, Valencia, Monty, and Laney tested their respective hypotheses and helped remove their obstacles in the process.

Randi discovered the repeated theme that she did not trust men. She knew she was attracted to men but realized how deep her distrust went as she talked with her coach. As a result, the initial step of her plan involved her going out on coffee dates with men, but making a continuous effort to do so with an open mind, realizing that she might at times distrust a good man, and at other times be attracted to a guy she shouldn't trust. With her eyes open, Randi started to date more frequently. She used her coaching sessions to learn how to accurately size up her dates and debrief herself, articulating her feelings about the experience, and addressing the negative feelings that could sabotage her. Dating regularly was a critical goal for Randi, and she achieved it faster than she thought possible.

For Valencia, an important coaching interaction involved exploring her accomplishments as a businesswoman. Though these accomplishments were significant, Valencia had minimized them in her own mind, perhaps believing that those business accomplishments paled with what a homemaker accomplished. In her coaching sessions, she was able to give herself a lot of credit for going against her father's negative view of women and conquering the business world. She pinpointed the behaviors at work that suggested she might not be leadership material—the tears, the shaky voice during presentations, the indecisiveness—and worked assiduously to eliminate them. Though she had tried in the past to get rid of them, she had failed. Now, with her understanding of why she acted this way in work situations, she was successful in stopping these counterproductive behaviors.

Monty got quite depressed when the harassment at work began. He started taking an antidepressant so he could sleep and function in the job. With the discovery of his Achilles factor—that he was put down as a boy the same way he was being harassed at work—he received compassion from his coach. This compassion was empowering; Monty needed someone to acknowledge and empathize with what he was feeling. He didn't feel as alone as he had in the past, and this connection gave him a base to move forward. Monty came to the realization that he should have the right to any career he chose. He then hired a human resource lawyer who met with the CEO of Monty's company. After that meeting, the harassment ceased. While some people no doubt continued to talk behind his back, Monty noticed that most people seemed more tolerant and accepting of who he was. People were now at least polite or quiet around him. His depression gradually faded away, and he found himself being more effective in his job—he had more energy and took more initiative. As a result he received a promotion within five months of starting his coaching sessions. His lawyer probably had helped things get better as well.

While working with her coach, Laney was surprised at how powerful the message of not being good enough was. She made peace with the fact that her mother spoke to her in those hurtful ways, but it was more important to Laney that she work toward her nursing degree. What she needed and had never had before was a structured series of goals that would provide her with mileposts to measure her progress toward a nursing degree. Achieving each small goal on the way to her degree—passing a tough class, completing an internship—counteracted the impact of her mother's words. This year she plans to graduate with honors from nursing school.

Never underestimate the power of Achilles factors or how they can stop you short of your goals. Use the coaching process to become aware of these factors and plan for their impact. Recognize, too, that dealing with these factors requires time and effort, that you and your coach first need to understand them, test the underlying hypothesis, and then use the hypothesis (assuming it proves valid) to achieve incremental next-step goals—working toward Big Goals and achieving breakthrough High-Energy Outcomes.

Refer to the following list, which summarizes the steps to take when managing Achilles factors:

Managing Achilles Factors

AWARENESS OF FACTOR

↓

HYPOTHESIS GENERATION

↓

HYPOTHESIS TESTING

↓

MANAGING FACTOR

↓

NEXT-STEP GOALS

↓

BREAKTHROUGH OUTCOMES

Please read the next Inspiration and complete this chapter's coaching exercise, The Obstacle Tackle Box. Refer to the client's sample exercise. Blog your thoughts in your journal or online.

DR. JOE'S INSPIRATION

"Welcome your biggest vulnerabilities, for they are the windows into your future greatness."

Full Life Exercise

The Obstacle Tackle Box: Uncovering Your Achilles Factors

Name what is blocking you (Achilles factor), state why you think this is happening (hypothesis), say whether you confirm your hypothesis, and state how you resume pursuit of your goals.

Achilles Factors	Hypothesis	Hypothesis Confirmed	Incremental Next Steps toward Outcome
		☐ Yes ☐ No	
		☐ Yes ☐ No	
		☐ Yes ☐ No	
		☐ Yes ☐ No	

NIGEL'S RESPONSE

Achilles Factors	Hypothesis	Hypothesis Confirmed	Incremental Next Steps toward Outcome
Decreased confidence	Mother constantly criticized me.	☒ Yes ☐ No	Manage my self-critical thoughts.
Am a black man in a white career	Subjected to discrimination frequently.	☒ Yes ☐ No	Keep pursuing my ambitions; persist.
Obesity	Subjected to nasty comments frequently.	☒ Yes ☐ No	Persist; be proud; manage weight with coach.

(continued)

Achilles Factors	Hypothesis	Hypothesis Confirmed	Incremental Next Steps toward Outcome
Workaholic	Told my job performance as a black man had to be better than others'.	☒ Yes ☐ No	Work with coach to emphasize ten other spheres.

NIGEL'S BLOG

I am pleased to finally address the issues I believe are holding me back. For a long time now, I realized that I was excessively criticized by my parent as a child. My mother was probably very damaged from discrimination, by poor parenting herself, and by some trauma, but she truly abused me emotionally with her constant criticisms. I am pleased that I finally am going to address my self-critical thoughts that have resulted from this abuse.

As a black man, I have experienced frequent discrimination from teachers, white friends and their families, and the workplace. This has left me with some shame and feeling like there is something wrong with me. I plan on working with my coach on going for my vision dreams and never giving up—and realizing that I am as worthy as anyone else.

Being overweight is the thing I am most ashamed of. As a boy, I felt so bad about myself, so all I did was eat to soothe the pain. But now I believe my obesity hurts my health, my social life, and my confidence. I am going to come up with a plan with my coach to manage my weight.

I work way too hard! My folks always instilled in me that I had to work twice as hard as anyone else because I am a black man. I am tired of this unfair standard for blacks. I am sick of seeing myself as a minority instead of an equal citizen. I am going to concentrate on the ten other spheres with my coach to get me out of the Work sphere.

CHAPTER 14

Approach Greatness

If you're like most people, you aspire to greatness. You don't just want a good career, you want one that provides tremendous satisfaction and financial rewards. You don't want to settle for an okay relationship, you want one that is enormously fulfilling. It may be that greatness, like perfection, is impossible to achieve. Approaching greatness, however, is a fair goal and one that coaching facilitates.

Approaching greatness means being the best you can be. It is hard work. There are obstacles. There must be accountability and humility. It is usually impossible to achieve it without assistance from others, including a coach. It's much easier to settle for being pretty good or average. Yet an astonishing number of people seek greatness in various areas of their lives. I suspect that you have these aspirations or you wouldn't have picked up this book; you would have been content to remain in therapy and not achieve your most ambitious goals. Perhaps your motivation involves the challenging times in which we live. As the economy toughens, as violent conflicts between countries continue, and as global warming accelerates, you become aware of the precariousness of existence and become focused on doing the best you can in the time you have. You may become fed up with the materialistic tendencies and trends out there and seek to simplify your life. Or you may seek a spiritual connection as the world seems to be going to hell in a handbasket. Whatever the motivation, you are driven to excel in one or more spheres to counteract the problems and challenges that arise.

Seeking greatness comes in many forms. You have to define what exactly it is for yourself, and your definition will probably be quite different from that of anyone else. As discussed, you need to examine your life in all eleven spheres and see what strengths and weaknesses you wish to optimize. This examination starts you on the road to greatness.

I find that most people need a coach to help them raise the bar and work toward what I referred to in previous chapters as the Spheres of Life Coaching Outcomes System (SOLCOS). It is this process that enables you to achieve your breakthrough High-Energy Outcomes, which are nothing more than ambitious goals that put you on the path to greatness. If you use the coaching tools I've described, such as Spheres of Life Coaching and the Achilles Plan, you will discover your authentic self and your personal truths. By connecting to these real aspects of your self, you can define a life that approaches greatness. Deciding what weaknesses to transform to strengths; deciding what spheres on which to concentrate; and deciding what strengths to further strengthen—these are all factors you will use to establish your personal goals regarding greatness.

Henry is someone who has approached greatness, though in recent years he was just about as far removed from greatness as anyone can be. An electrician for twenty years, married for fifteen years, and father of four children, he became increasingly irritable, lethargic, and disgruntled with life. He could not tell his wife how he was feeling. He just did not know how to put it into words. His productivity at work had fallen, and his supervisor was concerned. Henry engaged the services of a coach, who helped Henry discover that he was fine in many spheres, but he was very unhappy about working so much and missing out on spending time with his wife and family. This may seem obvious in the telling, but Henry had accepted the status quo. To him, no alternative existed to working hard and seeing his family only occasionally. It was just the way things were. The coach helped Henry see the alternatives, and they began to create a plan that made these alternatives realities. As a result of the plan, Henry convinced his wife to go on frequent one-to-one dates with him, and they also planned two major vacations with the kids every year. Within a few years these simple tactics improved Henry's mood—so much so that Henry's supervisor noticed. He especially noticed that Henry was not only happier at work but also much more productive. In the following year, Henry achieved other breakthrough High-Energy Outcomes related to his desire to be a more involved husband and father. For him, greatness was all about enjoying his family as much and as deeply as he could.

Can you approach greatness through coaching? Unlike therapy, coaching expects clients to be active participants in the process. If you go into coaching expecting your coach to do it all, you'll never approach greatness in any aspect of your life. You may do everything your coach suggests, but you'll just be going through the motions. For coaching to help you achieve your most ambitious outcomes, you have to do your part and often take the lead.

Strive for Mission and Purpose

What gives your life meaning? For each person, meaning is rooted in a particular set of values and activities. Some get involved in a socially oriented career, some discover a spiritual calling, some join an environmental cause, and some become active in charity. As a coach, part of my job is to help my clients find what is meaningful to them. Once they do, they are able to approach greatness, since mission and purpose give them targets to shoot for.

I would encourage you to search for your definition of mission and purpose, not once in a blue moon but as a continuous activity. Too often, we become bogged down in our ordinary daily activities and fail to look beyond the need to finish a project on time or go shopping or pick up the laundry. If you make a consistent effort to reflect on what gives your life purpose, you'll find that coaching will help you achieve your goals more readily than if you just keep your nose to the grindstone.

Later in this chapter, I discuss *white space thinking* (WST), in which you clear your mind completely and try to connect to something new and innovative—such as what gives your life its purpose.

Also, in writing your mission statement, consider that a mission is analogous to the software that drives a computer's hardware. This is what you need to discover about your mission. When you practice WST in respect to mission and purpose, use your journal to record your thoughts. You should eventually write a concise statement that defines words that are both clear and sound right to you. Your mission statement is your driver—make sure you review it often and check if you are on track. You can refer to the following table for a format to use in your journal or blog.

	Definition	Sample Responses
My mission	One's driver or overall objective	My mission is to help people with housing and health care needs.
My purpose in life	What is your intention in your life?	My intention is to help and challenge others to live a better life.

At fifty, Barney realized that his career was meaningless to him. He was a successful bond trader and by all outward appearances was a huge financial success. But what others did not realize was that he viewed himself as a failure. In his college years, he had wanted to study medicine, but his father convinced him to become a trader "just like your old man." Now he had two kids in college and a marriage of twenty-eight years.

Recently, as Barney's mood darkened, his wife kept asking him what was bothering him. Barney at first didn't know the answer. When he had some time to think about his reality, he realized that his thoughts were very self-critical and he had no sense of meaning in his day-to-day career. However, with coaching, it became increasingly clear that he still wanted to go to medical school. He realized it would be no fewer than ten years until he was finished with medical training, but he had come to understand that being a doctor was his authentic path; that it didn't matter how long it took or that he would never make as much money as a doctor as he did as a bond trader. In the coaching sessions, Barney grasped the fact that he might be the greatest bond trader the world had ever known, but he would never approach greatness, at least not in the larger sense of his definition of personal greatness. On the other hand, if in ten years Barney was a country doctor with a small practice and an equally small income, he could approach greatness because he was doing something authentic and meaningful to him. Currently, Barney is in medical school, on his way to becoming a physician, and happier and more purpose-driven than he has ever been.

In coaching, Barney used Spheres of Life Coaching to get clear on what he wanted to address in all the areas of his life. He put together an incremental next-step goal plan to work toward getting accepted to medical school. He took necessary post-baccalaureate coursework in the sciences and the necessary entrance examinations. His clear prioritization and goal-setting helped him achieve his breakthrough High-Energy Outcomes of attending medical school.

Pursue Passion, Playfulness, and the Pleasure Principle

Approaching greatness sounds like serious business, and it is in only one sense: that it will demand a lot from you to make it happen. But this is your life we're talking about, not simply an arduous task that must be done. Ironically, to achieve great things in your life through coaching, instead of elbow grease you'll require all the passion and playfulness you can muster. Your passion is the energy that fuels the entire process of turning your truth into your new reality. Your playfulness is your enthusiasm, your ability to have fun, be spontaneous and get excited—this approach will actually help you the most at designing the next authentic stage of your life and career.

If you find that coaching is drudgery, it's time to find a new coach. Your coach should make the entire process as positive and fun as possible, but you, too, need to focus on having fun as you learn and grow. If the process becomes too dull or painful, you'll probably quit short of your goals.

Luanne's husband, Elliot, constantly complained that their home was a mess. Luanne was ashamed of how she kept the home, especially after giving up her job to be a stay-at-home wife and mother—she felt she wasn't living up to the responsibilities of her new role. In coaching, I asked Luanne to approach the home tasks in a new way—with optimism, a sense of play, and fresh ideas. In her Achilles Plan she set the goals of hiring a home organizer, she bought and installed an outstanding sound system in the house to make task completion more pleasurable while listening to her favorite music, and she hired a designer to make physical changes in the home that would help with the organization.

The biggest surprise for Luanne was that the home improvement project became fun. She enjoyed working with the home organizer as everything became neater and put in its place. The designer made some clever changes, increasing storage capacity and eliminating the household clutter. All the while, Luanne listened to her music system as she worked on the house and found she could slip into a kind of meditative state as she listened and organized. She loved being able to listen and learn about classical music composers and soon supplemented her listening with symphony tickets; eventually she and Elliot bought a season series.

Elliot was appreciative and proud of how Luanne was adapting to her new role. They had agreed that it was important to have one stay-at-home parent until the kids reached early adolescence, and Luanne accepted that responsibility, even though she had enjoyed her job. Now she was learning how to become passionate and playful as she made a transition to a new part of her life. Over time, not only did Luanne find great satisfaction as a stay-at-home mom, but also her relationship with Elliot improved. She discovered, as many of my clients have, that improvement in one sphere often optimizes another sphere.

Be Creative

People often underestimate the importance of innovation in everyday life. However, it is vital to harness one's creativity and out-of-the-box thinking when working to optimize one's spheres. This is very challenging for most people. I call the mental space one gets in for innovation and creativity white space thinking (WST). (I called it "clear the slate" thinking in earlier writings.) It is vital for you to have completely fresh thinking about approaching a goal or an obstacle. You need to lose all your past assumptions and reassess your routines. Be open to alternatives. Remind yourself that just because you've always done something one way doesn't mean you need to do it that way in the future. Find an activity or environment that fosters your creativity. Going for a walk, meditation, and even exercise often help people enter into white space thinking. Think of what activity would foster WST for you.

For example, Theo wanted to open his own retail store—one of his goals was to run his own business. During coaching sessions, Theo often communicated how driven he was to open this store—he even dreamed about it—but then would raise all the reasons why it wasn't possible. When creating his business plan, for instance, Theo discovered that he couldn't afford the payments for his home as well as his new store. For a few weeks, Theo was stuck, but his coach encouraged him to move into WST. Theo decided to use running to move into that space. He had always found that the familiar motion allowed him to reflect and think about things differently. Normally, Theo listened to music while he ran, but he decided that he'd try running without music and concentrate on the obstacles to opening a store. As he ran, he happened to think about his late grandfather, an immigrant who lived above a corner grocery store with his family. It occurred to him that he might combine his living space with his working space. Within the week, he found the perfect space that met both requirements and sold his current residence. Would Theo have come up with this idea if he hadn't used WST? Possibly, but it might have taken him weeks or months to do so, and by then he might have given up on the possibility of affording his business.

WST is also used when a client knows he wants to design and implement something new in his life—whether a career, a house, a hobby, a life purpose, or even a relationship. For example, Kyle knew he wanted to change careers, but he didn't know what career he wanted to pursue. So Kyle's coach asked him to practice WST by making a list of up to ten possible careers that he might be willing to pursue. Then Kyle had to investigate each possibility and state its pros and cons from his perspective. His investigation could include reading about it; talking to experts about it; volunteering and doing it for a while; and even just imagining what it would be like. Kyle had to present the pros and cons of each career possibility to his coach for discussion.

Another trigger to WST is making mistakes that lead you to an unexpected thought or discovery. Most leaders will say that mistakes need to be valued in managers. This is one of the reasons stated frequently—because mistakes can trigger WST and therefore generate innovation.

Show Humility, Competence, and Integrity

Greatness is frequently associated with people who exhibit humility, competence, and integrity. Humility is often defined as respectful modesty. Recognizing that you serve others gives you the opportunity to form strong, long-lasting relationships that are crucial to achieving goals. Being humble also allows you to accept coaching suggestions without becoming defensive or resistant. You're more open to a coach's suggestion that you start a new career in an entry-level role or that you go to school to learn something critical for a goal. Keep in mind that humility has nothing to do with passivity per se. On the contrary, it can be associated with great power and effectiveness. For example, a person may help thousands in need by their charitable activities, and yet may see themselves completely in service to those they assist.

Humility often leads to your being appreciative and grateful for something in your life. Don't take anything for granted, and be appreciative for all good things. As you move through the coaching process, you're going to experience some pain and obstacles. When you have a base of appreciation—when you remind yourself of all the good things you have—it becomes much easier to deal with difficult experiences.

Competence is definitely part of greatness. When people work overtime to be excellent at some task or tasks, they are laying the foundation for greatness in some area of their life. Competence opens the door to future leadership. When people see that you are proficient at what you do, they tend to listen more to what you have to say.

Integrity means doing the right thing. Are my behaviors consistent with my values? If they are, then you are likely displaying integrity. If there is a contradiction, you will need to either revise your value that is contradicted or more likely change the behavior that contradicts your belief system and your principles for living. It is unlikely that a person in conflict with his or her own values is going to approach greatness. Your coach should demand integrity from you, knowing that if you're duplicitous or take shortcuts in any sphere, you're only going to achieve goals temporarily. You may lie and cheat your way to the top job in an organization, but that behavior will eventually sabotage your work goal (as well as goals in other spheres) because you will lose the respect of others (and of yourself). Alternatively, consider how a lack of integrity can impact your relationship goals.

Aiden was married for five years to Tia. During the first three years, their relationship couldn't have been better. But by accident, Aiden ran into his high school sweetheart, Adele, and they began an affair. The affair went on for two years before Aiden hired a coach to help him decide what to do. In coaching, Aiden realized that the affair violated his marital vows and his values of honesty and commitment. He grappled with the choice of leaving his wife for Adele or with coming clean and disclosing his affair to Tia. He chose the latter. She was obviously extremely upset and said that somehow she knew about the affair because of Aiden's emotional absence. After her tears, Tia gave Aiden a choice: stop seeing Adele immediately and start seeing a relationship coach together, or get divorced. Aiden took a walk, came back, and told Tia he would agree to couple coaching and stop seeing Adele. Aiden displayed integrity in his choice and one year later was more committed to Tia than ever. His new behaviors of greatness are built on honesty, integrity, humility, and appreciation. Being in sync with his values allowed him to make the right choices for himself.

Be Empowered

At one time or another we all wonder if we are as good as others. Are we as good an athlete? Do we have as much money? Are we as muscular? Are we as pretty? Are we as smart? Are we as funny? Moving from feeling less than to feeling equal to others is my definition of empowerment. True power is feeling equal to others. You can see the Taoist opposites in my definition of power and humility. True power is true humility, and true humility is true power. It's a fascinating relationship between these two states of being.

Empowerment is crucial for coaching to be effective. If you feel powerful without being arrogant, you're in an ideal position to take action on your coaching plan. You believe you can accomplish goals, yet you don't accomplish them by diminishing others. Greatness in any sphere can't be achieved without a positive sense of your own power; it also can't be achieved if you view your power as existing because others around you feel powerless; then your sense of power is insecure false power.

I am interested in empowerment of everyone, but I have a special interest in empowerment of all minorities because many minorities have been given the message that they are less important than others. Therefore, members of minorities are responsible for learning that they are equal to others. Coaching is one way they can learn this.

Isaac grew up in inner-city projects. As a boy, he was skinny and always terrified that he would be beaten up or accidentally shot in crossfire. In high school, he started to play football and baseball. He began to lift weights and bulk up. Soon he was quite muscular and fairly imposing to most people. The problem is that his increase in size didn't erase his inner feelings of vulnerability. So for years, Isaac felt diminished on the inside as he grew bigger and older. It was not until he was put on probation at his new job (for insulting others at the workplace) after college that he started to address his inner self with a coach. He discovered that because he grew up in a state of constant fear, he never formed a solid and safe sense of self. He continued to work on managing his thoughts about his worth and vulnerability. Soon he started to feel better about himself and his job performance rose rapidly. He was commended at work for being consistently respectful to others, which was a 180-degree turnaround. Isaac was empowered because he finally knew in his gut that he was equal to others and didn't have to put anyone down—and instead could enjoy the company of his colleagues.

Live by Your Values

Great leaders throughout history have been driven by their core beliefs or values, and people who get the most out of coaching also have a strong set of clear values. There are so many decisions and questions along the way where people can be thrown off the path toward their goals, and values help keep people on their path. When you have a strong system of beliefs, you can turn to them when you're confused. When you value honesty, you know that you need to be truthful with a boss, a spouse, or a friend, even though it's difficult to do so. Values help you maintain consistent, positive behaviors, and they guide you as you put a coaching plan into action and try out unfamiliar behaviors.

Other people tend to know whether you are a person who lives by his values. Remember that they witness your behaviors, so if you are talking the value and not walking the value, this discrepancy, perhaps hypocrisy, is noted. For example, we all know the politicians and religious leaders who judge others and are then exposed for doing a similar behavior. Usually this scenario occurs because their values are not deeply held and followed. For example, a politician may arrest citizens for criminal behavior. Often such a politician makes many enemies, so their behavior had better be squeaky-clean. But then amazingly, as we all have seen, the politician will get caught either doing the behavior he has judged and criticized, or break a law or other important rule.

The lesson here is that if you don't truly live by your values, you can be sure that you will get caught in some way, like the politicians who stray from their beliefs. Therefore it is vital to truly talk and walk your values if they are going to mean anything over time.

It is really important for you to clarify your key values because they serve as a foundation for your life going forward. If honesty, charity, interpersonal respect, education, kindness, wealth, or wellness ring true for you, I invite you to make a list of all your key values in each sphere. You can write this exercise in your journal and set it up as in the following figure:

Sphere	Key Values (examples)
Self	Calm, enlightenment, personal growth
Work	Meaning, contribution, calling, persistence
Love	Mutuality, kindness, passion, commitment
Family	Loyalty, ritual, celebration
Friends	Companionship, connection, laughter
Body	Sacredness, wellness, prevention, resilience, attractiveness
Community	Generosity, harmony, giving
Spirit	Humility, guidance, divinity, recovery
Money	Affluence, comfort, security
Fun	Playfulness, bliss, enjoyment, journeys
Home	Simplicity, safety, warmth, privacy, shelter

Manage Bad Habits and Addictions with Responsibility

It is your job to work on ownership of your life—past, present, and future. If you seek greatness, take complete responsibility for the cards you were dealt. You need to give up your victim mentality and take responsibility for the way things are—including bad habits and addictions—as we began discussing in chapter 3. No doubt you've known people who went to therapy for years and spent a great deal of time complaining to their therapist about the unfairness of a boss or how they were trapped in a job, a marriage, or a geographic location. They can complain about procrastination, spending too much money shopping, or drinking too much. Coaching is predicated on clients taking responsibility for managing their lives, so they need to assume that responsibility. Therefore, monitor yourself for victim-think and victim-talk: "If only it wasn't for . . . " is one common victim opening, as is "It's not my fault that . . . " or "There's nothing I can do about it . . . " In chapter 3, we began talking about how coaching can assist a client in managing an addiction or a bad habit. Here I want to expand on that theme and demonstrate how that very management can also be a path to enlightenment and personal greatness. We can look at bad habits and addictions in terms of the timeless story of Achilles' heel—when managed well, these vulnerable areas can stimulate achievement, self-awareness, accomplished goals, and even spiritual enlightenment—demonstrating that weaknesses *can* evolve into new strengths. However, when unmanaged, they can lead to a downward spiral—as occurred with the demise of the great Achilles.

Discipline is a kind of subset of responsibility, and from a coaching perspective it means taking a step-by-step approach to the coaching tasks at hand. This includes setting your Big Goals to achieve breakthrough High-Energy Outcomes, including the management of your issues, bad habits, and more serious addictions, if present. If you don't manage bad habits, they can hamper even the best coach's efforts. If your bad habit is to retreat into a shell in social situations, then develop social skills so you can relax and enjoy social interaction. If you are using drugs, then get in a program that will help you stop using them. If you are disorganized and lazy and can't get anything done, then make a conscious, concerted effort to impose order on your behaviors and energize yourself by setting small, realizable goals. If you are perpetually late, then learn how to be on time.

Managing bad habits takes a positive attitude and effort; you have to want to manage them, and you have to do something about them (rather than just thinking you *will* do something). Your coach can help you manage them by offering some tools and techniques, and if your habit is truly an addiction, he can suggest programs that might help.

Juanita drank alcohol since she was fifteen years old. She had started with beer in high school, and in college she began to binge more on weekends and added vodka to the mix. Despite her drinking, Juanita maintained excellent grades and upon graduation got an exciting job in a large bank. At first her boss was very impressed with her, but soon, due to her many absences, frequent lateness, and decreasing productivity, she was put on probation and told to hire a coach or she would be terminated. When she hired her coach she was in a lot of denial about her drinking. Too often, her drinking allowed her to cope with things that weren't going well in her life, such as her job and her relationships with her husband and children. It was only when she resolved to manage this habit—when she included the big goal of "manage alcohol" in her plan—that the coaching began to work. Her next-step goals included detoxing from alcohol, maintaining abstinence, going to Alcoholics Anonymous meetings every day for ninety days, and working with a sponsor on the 12 steps.

One year later, Juanita celebrated her one-year anniversary of abstinence from alcohol. She was able to see improvement in all spheres of her life, which placed her at the beginning of the path to greatness. She also received a promotion at work and praise from her boss. Quitting drinking doesn't get all the credit, but managing this bad habit allowed her to pursue her coaching goals without being distracted and derailed. Now the work really begins for Juanita to design a life of confidence and greatness.

Live Simply, Focus Intently, and Persist

People who follow these three principles often make rapid progress in coaching. This is as opposed to those who complicate their lives, who can't concentrate on important tasks, and who lack the will to see things through. People spend so much time making their lives complicated. To achieve true greatness, you must lead a simple life. By simple I don't mean rejecting all material things and living in the country or on a mountaintop. Simple means living your life according to your values and mission. As a result, you naturally prioritize what's important. You emphasize relationships over material things.

Simplicity gives you the energy to focus on your key coaching assignments. Rather than dissipate your time and effort on a hundred different tasks, you can concentrate on priority goals in whatever spheres are of greatest concern to you. Focus is the ability to concentrate with laserlike intensity on your Achilles Plan goals.

Focus is a vital life skill. In terms of the coaching experience, without it, it would mean being unable to concentrate on your Achilles Plan goals. Without focus, you would be unable to learn new things. You need to live a simple life so that you are calm, which, in turn, allows for improved concentration.

Regarding persistence, I've said it before and I'll say it again: coaching doesn't work instantly. You have to be stubbornly persistent, moving past setbacks and failures, to achieve your goals. In fact, your persistence will allow you to learn from setbacks and failures, and you'll use these negative events as motivations. I teach that persistence is one of the most powerful tools in life and on the road to greatness. Never giving up is a great strategy for life success as well as for weathering a few mistakes and bad fortunes along the way.

Brooke started a natural-paper stationery store two years ago. After one year in business she almost closed her doors because she went into debt as business was slow. A friend suggested that she hire a coach who might help her give the business one last try. She began seeing the coach, who referred her to a marketing specialist, and together the three of them developed a strategy and action plan to increase revenues. The plan required a great deal of time and additional financial investment on Brooke's part. Many people would have looked at that investment of time and money and said no, but Brooke trusted her coach and, more importantly, trusted her gut. She knew her business could be viable if she just got the formula right. Her conviction that she had the right business idea and the right plan allowed her to persist despite two years of being in the red. By the end of year three, Brooke was ecstatic that her revenues had doubled in one year. She had implemented the marketing strategy and was seeing results. Focus and persistence were paying off!

Avoid Burnout and Build Resilience

Greatness can't be approached if you give up or burn out. I realize that my clients face significant challenges and that there are going to be times when they are tempted to say, "I can't do this anymore." Burnout is a possibility in any sphere. You can decide you're never going to lose weight or that you'll never become a spiritual person. You may have tried for a week, a month, or a year, but at some point you feel burned out from the effort. Burnout actually mimics the symptoms of depression, but it is clear that external stressors cause burnout.

Recognize and prevent symptoms of burnout. These can include sleep problems; hopelessness; less interest in hobbies; and low levels of confidence, energy, and concentration. They are related to external stressors, such as a difficult boss, marital problems, a sick child, poor wellness practices, or loss of a parent. You can treat burnout with a Spheres of Life coaching inquiry into what is working and what is not and using your Achilles Plan goals to get back in better balance. Maintaining your life balance also allows you to avoid burnout. Usually, doing your incremental next-step goals in all spheres can move you back into a state of resiliency. Sometimes medication is necessary as well if the burnout symptoms are severe.

Interestingly, if you keep working on your goals, you will find that you can even surpass the state of resilience and move into the state of optimal performance as discussed. The temporary weakness of burnout can therefore be transformed into resilience, and sometimes even new breakthrough High-Energy Outcomes can be achieved.

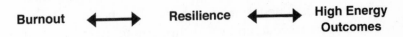

Burnout ⟷ **Resilience** ⟷ **High Energy Outcomes**

Build Confidence

The nice thing about working toward greatness is that the process tends to increase your self-confidence. Pushing the envelope in all your spheres opens you up to your possibilities and potential. You feel hopeful and optimistic because you experience yourself getting closer and closer to your mission and outcomes.

This isn't to say that if you enter the coaching milieu, you'll automatically be confident. If your life is not aligned with your personal truth, you will have doubts. If your life is not aligned with your mission and purpose, you will possess no confidence or a false confidence. In fact, as discussed in earlier chapters, when clients start out in coaching, they frequently are uncertain about their own ability to achieve any significant goal. They come in beaten and bloodied by life, so it can take time to gain confidence as part of the coaching process.

Amy was a homemaker, married ten years with three kids. Her family was the envy of all. Amy and her husband, Jackie, were an attractive couple, and both were quite successful in their careers. Jackie was a school custodian, and Amy ran a bridal boutique in town. All seemed fine on the surface. Underneath, however, Amy had become quite depressed. She couldn't talk to anyone about what was going on until she hired a coach. In doing an honest inquiry with the Spheres of Life Coaching, Amy realized that her biggest misalignment with her truth was that she was in denial about being a lesbian. She had recently had a short-lived affair and realized that she needed to be with a woman. At the same time, she was terrified about what that would mean for her family. She was trying to find a way to tell Jackie and discuss her true feelings, but she lacked the confidence that she could do so without destroying her life and the lives of those she loved. Amy recognized that if she acted on her feelings she would be vilified by others; judged; and most importantly, hurt Jackie and her family. It took her weeks working with a coach to formulate her Big Goals in the Achilles Plan, which provided incremental next-step goals to communicate the truth to Jackie and others as caringly as possible. Having a method gave Amy confidence, and eventually she took the first step, coming out to Jackie and her parents.

Coming to terms with one's truth does not mean it's going to be easy or that you need to act on anything right away. It simply means you have greater integrity with yourself as well as with others, which enables you to be aligned with your values, mission, meaning, and purpose. How you disclose and act on these truths is completely up to you and relates to your other values, such as honesty, kindness, and respect.

So many people come to coaching complaining of self-critical thoughts and low levels of confidence. Most commonly they are bright, talented, attractive, and dynamic people who really ought to be confident. But for many reasons they are not. They feel they are a failure in some of the spheres, and they feel they disappointed others in their life, including mates, families, and themselves. But confidence is achieved in coaching when one works hard to achieve his goals in all areas but also when one allows himself to be human and imperfect. Life balance results from multidimensional goal completion but also in embracing one's humanness, one's mistakes, and one's failures. Also, deeply realizing that one is equal to all others—empowerment—gives one a huge boost of confidence. Out of the celebration of achieving breakthrough High-Energy Outcomes and the forgiveness of one's own imperfection and failings, confidence can be born—it can thrive into the future or in a new environment.

Please read the next Inspiration and complete the chapter's coaching exercise, Approaching Greatness. Refer to the client's sample exercise. Blog your thoughts in your journal or online.

DR. JOE'S INSPIRATION

"Aspiring to greatness is daunting for most of us because it requires us to be at our most humble and most competent at the same time."

Full Life Exercise

Approaching Greatness

Write what each sphere would look like if you were approaching greatness in that sphere.

Sphere	For Me, Approaching Greatness Would Look Like This in Each Sphere:
Self	
Work	
Love	
Family	
Body	
Friends	
Community	
Spirit	
Money	
Fun	
Home	

ANGELO'S RESPONSE

Sphere	For Me, Approaching Greatness Would Look Like This in Each Sphere:
Self	I would be confident and at peace with my progress in all the ten other spheres.
Work	Work would align with my mission, meaning, and purpose. I would have achieved goals in my career that would make me proud.
Love	I would approach a place with my mate where I am far more joyful about giving than receiving.
Family	I would be in a place where I can love the greatness in my family members and forgive the weaknesses, since I have them as well.
Body	I would be honoring my wellness on a level as never before: optimal nutrition, exercise, care of health, and body image.
Friends	I would delight in my circle of close friends.
Community	I would be involved in activities that enhance the community; I would volunteer some hours every week.
Spirit	I would nurture my spirit through personal prayer, meditation, and the study of different religions.
Money	I would have enough money so I wouldn't worry about it as much.
Fun	I would have tons of laughter and fun with friends and family.
Home	Home would be simple, with little clutter, and quite comfortable, with some cool electronics.

ANGELO'S BLOG

It is exciting to even imagine what greatness looks like. I know it isn't attainable, but it can be a trip trying to get there! I am most excited about being confident and at peace, having met or nearly met many of my life goals, which include having a career that is finally aligned with my mission; becoming a good lover or learning to love; finding peace with family; a dedication to wellness; connection to friends; giving back to the community; evolution of my spirit; peace with money and material possessions; and tons of fun.

CHAPTER 15

A Better Life and a Better World

A *great* life. Sounds good, doesn't it? Even a *better* life sounds good. But why not go for the great life? For most people in therapy, the answer is that a great life is not part of the process. You may gain insight into your behaviors and appreciation for events that shaped you, but greatness doesn't enter the equation. You are there to talk, and the assumption is that after a considerable time, you may use what you learn to diminish your problems.

These are modest aspirations, and if you fall within the broad range of normal, they are overly modest. Coaching aims higher, and it gives you tools to hit the target. In this book I have discussed how normal people can use coaching to aspire to the life they deeply desire. You can set big goals, incrementally implement changes, and build the life you want. Coaching allows you to work toward changing behaviors while you enjoy yourself more along the way.

I want normal people to have a way of pursuing their personal work without the pathologizing of the traditional therapy process. Everyone who embarks on this kind of work should be affirmed for doing it. This isn't just positive thinking. While I advocate optimism and forward thinking, I also believe that happiness and satisfaction resulting from coaching require vision, goal-setting, and the hard work it takes to land outcomes.

As I stated early on, this by no means is an anti-therapy book. Instead, it is a pro-coaching book, proclaiming an emerging field whose time has come. Again, I have huge respect for the training of therapists, but I do believe that a revolution of technique and philosophy is necessary. Therapists who treat normal people must become more clientcentric and more outcome-oriented. They also must become more multidimensional, recognizing that Self is only one of eleven spheres. They need to be willing to refer their clients to other professionals if they lack expertise in a given area.

And coaches need to consider obtaining clinical training so they can understand normal human development, and the basics of clinical treatment of mental illness and addictions. Over a period of time, most coaches will need to deal with these issues and must be familiar with symptoms and solutions.

Burt is president and founder of a video game company. He engaged the services of a coach, Dennis, to help him become a better leader and raise company revenues. However, in the early sessions it became clear to Dennis that Burt had some significant problems that would have to be addressed before progress in coaching could be made: Burt was depressed (not sleeping, not concentrating, not enjoying himself, feeling guilty, not eating well); paranoid (thought people were against him); had several untreated medical problems (high cholesterol, diabetes); and was terrified of people discovering that he was having a secret affair with a woman his daughter's age. So Dennis had to address these symptoms before Burt could begin the executive coaching. If they weren't addressed first, Burt would try to hide his problems and end up sabotaging the process. Therefore, Dennis referred Burt to a primary care physician to help with the medical problems and to a psychiatrist to deal with the depression and the paranoia. Once these problems were being managed, Dennis started to coach Burt. It was only at this point that Burt was capable of focusing on his leadership, business issues, and secret affair. Without dealing with the issues in other spheres, Burt's attention would have been elsewhere; his energy would have been devoted to nonbusiness matters; and he would have responded to coaching suggestions and plans halfheartedly.

In coaching, people are capable of great leaps up the ladder of life satisfaction, but they need to approach that ladder with an understanding of weaknesses and strengths, a vision, a plan, and a willingness to make changes holistically rather than narrowly. They also need to understand just how wide-ranging coaching's benefits can be—how it can be useful not only for individuals but also for organizations, communities, and nations. I'll talk about these wide-ranging benefits in a bit, but first I want to emphasize the attitude that best facilitates the coaching process.

Live in the Moment with a Plan

Wise people throughout history have observed that living in the moment is a major component of happiness. Some of this wisdom revolves around the concept of nirvana, clearing the mind of all thoughts, and how this state contributes to helping people feel alive, positive, and powerful. Living in the moment reveals that therapy shouldn't be such a serious pursuit. As discussed earlier, the famous British analyst and pediatrician D. W. Winnicott taught, playfulness is vital to enjoying the moment as well as for normal development to occur. This continues throughout the life cycle. When playfulness stops, development and change cease. Too often, therapy feels like drudgery to patients and is overly serious. People are in therapy for the same reason people eat their greens—they believe it's good for them, even if they often don't really enjoy it. However, with coaching, the client can work hard and thoroughly enjoy the experience. Though coaching isn't all fun and games, you should leave your sessions energized. You should feel challenged. Every so often you should have a smile on your face, for you have expanded your horizons through playfulness and laughter.

In addition to playfulness and nirvana, creativity and life planning are vital for achieving the outcome of a life you want. What sets this book apart from the well-meaning but pie-in-the-sky school of positive thinkers is that coaching offers a coherent, integrated, and well-organized method of inquiry, strategy, goal implementation, and outcome achievement. This incremental implementation of your vision is what moves coaching to another level of personal and organizational change. People need help implementing and maintaining change, not just being positive. The collaboration between you and your coach should yield innovative ideas, insights, and actual changes. Your coach should stimulate you to think in fresh ways about your history, your present, and your future. Your coach should also bring a creative spark to the strategic and outcome-oriented process.

Each coach has different tools. In these pages, I've presented the tools that I've developed and know are effective: the techniques, which include the Spheres of Life Coaching for multidimensional coaching and the Achilles Plan for reaching breakthrough High-Energy Outcomes—all comprising the key components of the Spheres of Life Coaching Outcomes System (SOLCOS).

Rather than concentrate on the negatives of therapy, I urge you to focus on the positives of coaching. Beyond just talk, coaching can be an approach that helps you figure out what is bothering you and what you can do about these issues, what your strengths are, and then what your goals are and how you can reach and implement these aspirations. If you're struggling with whether coaching would be a better option than therapy for you, here are three more simple questions that will help you make the decision:

- Am I normal or do I have symptoms of an active psychiatric problem such as depression or bipolar disorder?
- Does it seem as if at least some of the issues I'm grappling with exist in the ten spheres other than Self?
- Do I need a process that will get me out of therapy and get me moving in the direction I want my life to go?

If you answered yes to these questions, you're ready to take advantage of a groundbreaking, multidimensional coaching approach. In the process, you'll benefit from the power of the accountability relationship with your coach. As do the finest athletes, you will perform at your highest with the right coach.

Finding the right coach is not as difficult as it sounds. Earlier, I provided a number of suggestions for finding a coach that should facilitate the search process. Keep in mind that unlike finding one true love, there are many coaches who can help you. You may need a combination of coaches or a team of experts—a life coach, a business mentor, and a fitness coach, for instance.

Remember, too, that the coach you find may have a different process than the one this book advocates. That's fine as long as it makes sense to you and it's not the traditional therapy process. Any process that is multidimensional, action-focused, and goal-oriented should help.

Coaching is a process whose time has come. If therapy was perfectly positioned for people's issues in the twentieth century, coaching is ideally suited to today's zeitgeist.

Universal Values and a Refusal to Judge

As the world shrinks because geographic distance is no longer an issue; as the civil rights of minorities and all other people continue to advance in many countries; as interest in organized religion decreases and as interest in universal values increases; and as trends and events evolve, coaching is positioned perfectly to help people deal with these changes. Values that were traditionally under the auspices of religions are now under the auspices of nations, states, communities, employer groups, and individuals. Values such as interpersonal respect and belief in true equality for all (zero tolerance for activities such as racism and other forms of bigotry) are now being owned by many individuals when they create their own value systems. People are looking inward and outward to define the values that are important to them, and coaching provides a sanctuary for discussing these values.

Coaching, unlike therapy, is judgment-free. Judgment has caused more wars and conflict than any other maladaptive human behavior. Judgment of others is often a primitive method to cope with insecurity, envy, or frustration—usually disguised behind arrogance and superiority. Obviously, this conflicts with the universal value that all people are equal. Coaching facilitates new ways of getting along, supporting others, and making compromises—all vital outcomes. By decreasing judgment, coaching optimizes relationships, communities, nations, religious tolerance, and mutual respect.

In short, coaching fits with many people's needs in our current environment. If you're like most people, you want to discuss and define your values, to determine what really matters to you, and to use these values as guides for your life. If you're like most people, you also want to become aware of and manage your biases and assumptions that cause you to dismiss and diminish others unfairly. With strong values and a judgment-free perspective, you're in a much better position to succeed in the twenty-first century as diversity and universal values take root.

Optimize Organizations

Though I've emphasized individual coaching in this book, please be aware that this process is applicable to organizations. In fact, in some ways coaching is even more effective within an organizational context, since management endorses coaching and confers immediate credibility. When I've worked in organizations, people often get it right away. They see the value of coaching and are motivated to commit themselves to being coached. They don't have to fire their therapist and go through a period of indecision before they begin their coaching sessions.

If you think about it, organizational coaching isn't that different from coaching that involves spheres outside of Work. Typically,

I'll work with a high-level executive who isn't performing up to expectations or who is having trouble working with colleagues. He or she also has Achilles factors holding them back from performance goals—for example, a salesperson who is unable to close a big deal because he grew up in a home environment where cutting criticism was the rule, making him risk-averse. Such an executive needs to work with his coach to break through his old fears and set new performance goals. He too needs to create a vision for himself within the organization and from a larger career standpoint. He also needs to formulate incremental and larger goals and create a plan to work toward them.

Having coached everyone from CEOs to vice presidents to managers, I can tell you that the process is remarkably similar to coaching individual clients who have no organizational affiliation. People experiencing problems at work are facing issues in other spheres. It's not unusual to find a manager whose work has slipped because he's going through a divorce or because she's spiritually adrift. As I've noted, what happens in one sphere impacts what happens in another.

The Spheres of Life Coaching Outcomes System (SOLCOS) also can be applied on an organizational basis. By helping organizations understand and focus on strengths and weaknesses, values, mission and purpose, vision, goals, and outcomes, coaches also help improve the bottom line because of increases in productivity, employee retention, community involvement, and optimization of customer service.

Organizations require coaching on issues involving waste, pollution, global warming, terrorism threats, management, and employment; all are very important to the public at large. Organizations need someone to talk to them about corporate values and beliefs about public responsibility and community involvement. A coach can provide a process to help organizational leaders and employees define their beliefs and determine how to translate those beliefs into strategy and goal implementation. A coach also can help companies interested in "walking the talk" of mission and values, providing accountability and monitoring of these issues.

Communities and Nations

Coaching can affect communities and nations. By asking each citizen to work on himself or herself to approach greatness, communities and nations can both benefit from people who are taking responsibility for themselves and working with the SOLCOS to achieve what they want in life. This may seem like an overly idealistic or even naive assumption, but people need help in a world that is increasingly volatile, unpredictable, ambiguous, and diverse. It's confusing out there, and the more people are confused, the more useful coaching is for shining a light and illuminating a path.

Today, prejudice against those who are different remains a problem everywhere. Coaching, with its insistence on true equality, while coming to terms with events in the past that create prejudice, can serve an important social purpose. At the same time, though, the power of coaching tends to spread by word of mouth. It really is a grassroots movement that is establishing a strong foundation in cities throughout the United States and the world.

At a time when many people are less religious or less willing to listen to authority figures in government or corporations, they need someone to turn to for guidance. It's not a coincidence that the coaching movement has taken off in recent years. People are turning to coaches for guidance, while in the past they were more likely to turn to ministers, therapists, or even their bosses.

Communities and nations face huge challenges today, from diversity-based conflicts to choices between economic gain and environmental preservation. Coaching offers leaders of countries and communities a way to facilitate meeting these challenges. I don't know about you, but I certainly would feel better if the leaders of our country (as well as the leaders of other nations) had a coach offering a fresh perspective and feedback as well as working to create an effective plan and goals (and holding leaders accountable for their achievements).

Coaching is the result of a natural evolution in an era that has become increasingly complex and challenging. A coach can help individuals or much larger groups navigate a path through these confusing times.

Achieve Longevity

Though I have no hard scientific data to back me up, I'm convinced that most people will probably live longer and healthier lives by utilizing the SOLCOS. Coaching facilitates moving into optimal life balance over time. The body sphere goals assure that you will maintain a powerful wellness orientation, including such things as nutrition, exercise, body image, and care of health. More than that, coaching addresses all areas of life. Feeling healthy spiritually, having fun, and enjoying a meaningful career all contribute to our overall health. Whether you call it a holistic approach or multidimensional, coaching addresses the full range of issues people face and offers a plan to address these issues. People are frustrated if all they can do is talk about their lack of spirituality or their desire to have more fun. However, when you give them things they can do to achieve these goals, it's far more satisfying and stress-reducing.

Research suggests that everything from physical fitness to stress reduction to developing a spiritual connection helps people live longer. My belief, based purely on experience and observation, is that positive work in each of the spheres contributes to well-being. By and large, the people I've worked with or who I know who have lived to a ripe old age are those with a greater sense of fun; who are contributing members of a community; who have a strong circle of friends; and who have a healthy family life.

My theory is that unaddressed problems in any sphere can potentially take years off your life. While this theory is most obviously true when it comes to the Body sphere, it pertains to every area of life. When you feel unfulfilled in any area, it creates tremendous stress. If you long to have a great, meaningful relationship but are unable to establish it, you can work out in the gym until the cows come home and still feel the stress of this relationship absence.

On the other hand, when you've addressed your issues and goals in each sphere, you've probably done a terrific job of managing all the stress in your life. This doesn't guarantee that you'll live to be a hundred, but it certainly increases the odds that you won't be the victim of a stress-related disease.

SOLCOS ➡ **BALANCE** ➡ **LONGEVITY**

Cementing Outcomes

At the end of this chapter, you'll find a very important coaching exercise called Cementing Outcomes, for you to document your coaching achievements. It is the culmination of the coaching experience, providing you with a powerful reminder of what outcomes you have achieved in each sphere of life. I recommend that you use this exercise at least every six months. It is a way for you to document your progress and then go on to new challenges. It is important for you to give yourself credit for all your achieved outcomes. It is a lot of fun to celebrate these accomplishments.

Please read the next Inspiration and complete the chapter's coaching exercise, Cementing Outcomes. Refer to the client's sample exercise. Blog your thoughts in your journal or online.

DR. JOE'S INSPIRATION

"Working toward humility and greatness will truly transform the world into a place of playful creativity and regard for others."

Full Life Exercise

Cementing Outcomes

Write the outcomes you have achieved, and document the spheres
to which they belong.

Achilles Plan—Big Goals	Sphere

FABI'S RESPONSE

Achilles Plan—Big Goals	Sphere
Moved into new home	Home
Started new business	Work
Reinvigorated marriage	Love
Hanging out with best friends weekly	Friends
More confident from accomplishing goals	Self
Took two big trips this year	Fun
Found a congregation I enjoy attending	Spirit
Lost twenty pounds from eating better and working out daily	Body
Visit parents twice per year	Family

FABI'S BLOG

I am thrilled to record my accomplishments over the past six months. I am very proud that I moved into a new home, started an exciting clothing boutique business, went to couples counseling so my marriage is a lot of fun again, am spending time with friends frequently, took several terrific vacations, found this fantastic church for Sundays, lost twenty pounds!!! by cutting down on carbs and junk food, work out almost every day, and am in better touch with my folks. Best of all, I feel more confident.

Conclusion

This book is designed to offer you an alternative to therapy and to facilitate your coaching experience. No matter what spheres of life you choose to address, I hope you enjoy working toward the vision of your life.

Many of you, I suspect, will be drawn to coaching for a range of reasons. We have demonstrated that some seek greatness, some seek purpose, and others seek confidence. I have seen coaching enable all sorts of people to achieve incredible results. It's a process whose time has come, and I encourage you to take full advantage of it if you're a person with hopes and dreams that are part of most normal people's lives.

Congratulations! You have now gotten more in touch with your truths; you have decided whether or not to fire your therapist; you have learned a lot about coaching as applied to normal people; you have completed multiple coaching exercises; and you have learned from the many inspirations, questions, and quizzes.

Coaching usually doesn't work miracles, but in its ability to help people deal with difficulties and plan breakthrough opportunities, it often seems miraculous.

I wish you joy and adventure as you discover the formula for the next phase of your life.

Contact Dr. Siegler at

- Email: info@FLCenters.com
- Book: www.FYTbook.com
- Full Life Coaching Centers: www.FLCenters.com

INDEX

258

Index